Essay Writing for Adolescents with Language and Learning Difficulties

Essay Writing for Adolescents with Language and Learning Difficulties is a step-by-step guide for educators teaching secondary students with language difficulties how to write an English essay and, more importantly, how to do this on their own.

Essay writing is one of the most difficult skills that secondary school students need to develop, though there are limited resources available to support these students and their teachers. Based on research into language disorders in adolescence and language processing, the strategies in this book are easy to apply and represent a scaffolded and sequenced approach to teaching essay writing. The book's structure encourages students' skills and confidence to be developed gradually, each chapter building on the last, beginning with the early stages of text analysis and progressing through to writing a complete essay. While written with students with language difficulties in mind, the strategies in this book are applicable to teaching all secondary school students.

Written by a speech pathologist with over a decade's experience working in secondary schools, this book is an essential resource for all high school English teachers and any education professionals responsible for teaching adolescents how to write essays competently and confidently.

Kim Knight has worked as a speech pathologist for over a decade, practising in schools across Australia. She has a passion for books, and her degrees in English literature have proved invaluable in supporting secondary and university students struggling with narrative and essay writing.

Essay Writing for Adolescents with Language and Learning Difficulties
Practical Strategies for English Teachers

Kim Knight

First published 2022
by Routledge
4 Park Square, Milton Park, Abingdon, Oxon OX14 4RN

and by Routledge
605 Third Avenue, New York, NY 10158

Routledge is an imprint of the Taylor & Francis Group, an informa business

© 2022 Kim Knight

The right of Kim Knight to be identified as author of this work has been asserted in accordance with sections 77 and 78 of the Copyright, Designs and Patents Act 1988.

All rights reserved. No part of this book may be reprinted or reproduced or utilised in any form or by any electronic, mechanical, or other means, now known or hereafter invented, including photocopying and recording, or in any information storage or retrieval system, without permission in writing from the publishers.

Trademark notice: Product or corporate names may be trademarks or registered trademarks, and are used only for identification and explanation without intent to infringe.

British Library Cataloguing-in-Publication Data
A catalogue record for this book is available from the British Library

Library of Congress Cataloging-in-Publication Data
A catalog record for this book has been requested

ISBN: 978-1-032-20394-2 (hbk)
ISBN: 978-1-032-20393-5 (pbk)
ISBN: 978-1-003-26340-1 (ebk)

DOI: 10.4324/9781003263401

Typeset in Bembo
by Apex CoVantage, LLC

For Joy

Contents

Preface   ix
Acknowledgements   xi

Introduction   1
How This Book Began   1
About Adolescents With Language and Learning Difficulties   2
Memory, Processing and Schemas   7
So, What Now?   12

1   A Way to Analyse Texts   17
Identifying Themes   18
The Text + Theme Schema   21
Analysing Themes in Texts   25

2   Essential Essay Structures   44
English Essay Structure   44
The Body Paragraph   45
Texts and Excerpts for Practice   52

3   Essay Topic Breakdown and Planning   65
Basic 'One Way' Strategy   66
Agree/Disagree Strategy   72
Divide and Conquer Strategy   77
Incorporate Strategy   84

4   Writing an English Essay   91
Introductions   91
Conclusions   93
Putting It All Together   95
Exams   101
Final Words (for Students)   102

Appendix 105

Text-type, Genre, Theme Definitions 106
Sample Goals for Individual Learning Plans 107
Some Oral Language Supports 109
Text + Theme Schemas 110
Basic Narrative Schema 116
Cause and Effect Schema 117
Body Paragraph ACCESS Scaffold 118
PREP Introduction Scaffold 119
PS Conclusion Scaffold 120
Pronouns 121
Verb Tenses 122
Incorporated Strategy Synonyms 123
Selection of Summarised Texts 124
Copy of Fairy Tales 127
Short Stories for Extra Practice 129

Index 133

Preface

The idea that the best writing should flow through you effortlessly and end up a polished masterpiece on the page is very romantic. It's also a bit unhelpful, but we just can't seem to shake the notion that the ability to write well is some innate, free-flowing process that people either have or don't.

Typical language users who speak reasonably well don't consciously think much about how they do this. They often write reasonably well, and if not, then they have the skills to go back, edit and shape what they've written for clarity. To them, this feels routine. Their language processes were acquired and practised throughout their lives without any major interruptions along the way. Language seems to come to them naturally and automatically. However, it's not always that effortless. Language is not that simple.

Language needs structure. If we don't place sounds in words, words in sentences and sentences into paragraphs in a particular order, then we are incomprehensible. For typically developing students, language emerges with not much conscious effort on their part, or their teacher's part. Presumably they have the memory, attention and hearing faculties, and the environment and opportunities to support the acquisition of typical language, and that's why it all seems so unconstrained.

Students with language and learning disorders often struggle with acquiring and using age-appropriate vocabulary and sentence structures. Individuals might also lack the attention, memory and cognitive processes necessary to communicate age-appropriately. Because of underlying difficulties, they will often struggle to read and interpret academic texts and write about them.

Anything you can provide to support language for someone who has little structure is helpful. By scaffolding for struggling students you're providing them with deliberate and explicit representations of what typical language learners already have. And while the use of scaffolding and explicit teaching structures alone might not make struggling students deeply insightful readers and writers (although they might surprise you), it will provide them with the tools they need to express their thoughts through clear and organised language and writing.

This book is not designed to be a solution to every language learning difficulty faced by students who struggle with oral and written language. And it's not my intention to promote one type of learning or teaching theory over another. It is a resource to support the production of the most gruelling task required of English students, the English essay. It is not a programme but a series of scaffolds, schemas and strategies you can work through sequentially, or apply individually.

Adolescent students with language and learning difficulties are often put at the end of waiting lists for specialist services or asked to see tutors. This can be because specialists are unaware of the prevalence of language and learning difficulties or might lack the tools to assist adolescents who present with these difficulties. Misinformation and inexperience also allow prevailing attitudes to flourish; thinking that the ship has sailed, and it's too late. But it's never too late to support people who struggle with language and learning.

Adolescents with developmental language disorder often slip through the cracks because their grades consistently fall below average in the classroom, but sometimes they do not test low enough on standardised language assessments to receive special assistance or funding. They know what they want to say but can't find the words. They put in the effort, but their grades don't improve. They're the students who have good ideas but fail to get them down on paper. They are the overwhelmed and overlooked, the often disappointed. This book is for these students, their equally overwhelmed teachers, tutors and support staff and the speech pathologists who work with all of them.

Acknowledgements

A special thank you to Mary-Ruth Mendel and Alexandra Ling who mentored me as a new speechie, and who continue to embolden and inspire—I'm still in awe of you both. My appreciation to the team at Taylor and Francis, including Vilija Stephens and Georgia Oman for their editorial support. Thanks to Jo Antareau for editing my earlier draft. Christine Payne and Naomi Knight, thank you for casting your eagle eyes over my proof copy. Any errors in the final publication are entirely my own. And finally, I thank my husband for his patience and encouragement, cups of tea and for his unwavering (if confounding) faith in my abilities.

Introduction

How This Book Began

When I started in private practice, I was working with school-aged students in all grades, providing one-to-one therapy and supplementing this with classroom strategies. I expected I'd be working mainly in early literacy, and with primary school students with speech or language disorder and that I'd see the occasional student for stuttering treatment. I expected to address difficulties with word finding, sentence structure, following directions, the usual. And I worked with those students, but I also worked with more upper primary and high school students than ever before. The older students presented with similar issues, but it didn't take long to see this cohort was unique.

For adolescents, I set about applying the strategies I'd used with the younger students. Obviously, there were greater demands on more abstract language for older students, and so I increased the complexity of the activities. I applied various strategies with goals to build vocabulary, improve comprehension and retention, and support them to process abstract concepts. For literacy, I used Writing Approach to Reading and Spalding methods. But the students I worked with wanted more discourse level support to write their assignments.

Unlike the younger students, who'd benefitted from skill-based intervention, targeting things like regular plurals or adjectives in isolation did not support the types of gains upper primary and secondary students, and their teachers, wanted to see. Language at this age, even when lower than typical, is still more advanced than lower primary. There are many shifts: concrete to abstract, learning to read versus reading to learn, and writing recalls and book reports slowly falls away in favour of writing arguments and essays. The tasks become more complex, and the workload increases. And even though these students needed underlying language skills, I knew this couldn't be the only goal.

I learned that the older students who came through my door had less time and a huge workload. They had their own ideas about the types of tasks they wished to improve. Therapy had to be relevant. They needed to experience some modicum of success within the first session, and if they couldn't, then they needed to know change was possible. They had to see the change happen. Unlike play-based therapies with little ones who are often oblivious there's work involved, the older cohort know why they're there, and if they were

DOI: 10.4324/9781003263401-1

sitting in front of me with a will to improve and didn't, I lost them. They needed to see the end point, the aim of the sessions, the reason for turning up.

I asked older students what they wanted to improve and heard the same things over again: to get better marks in English, get ideas on paper, write essays—this last one often followed by an eye roll or grimace.

These revelations prompted some digging, not only into adolescent language but also into the language and comprehension processes of typically developing adults and young people. I wanted to understand how typically developing adolescents acquired language, and what was happening when they presented with disordered language.

Getting student feedback was essential to buy-in, and crucial in goal setting and measuring outcomes. Conversations led to goals and planning centred on tasks rather than skills or domains. This is not to say that underlying skills (like syntax) or domains (like writing) weren't addressed; sometimes we'd spend entire sessions doing nothing but writing sentences, but they were embedded in a school-relevant task. Skill development was not the goal but the means to the end. We were still building the parts to form a whole, but we had the whole in mind at every step. Formulating goals according to tasks also proved easier to transition and measure in a classroom, and easier to place into an individual learning plan.

I developed the schemas and strategies in this book over time to scaffold the essay writing process for the adolescent students I worked with. The task was chosen based on student demand, and the strategies are reproduced here so teachers, speech pathologists and other professionals can apply them to support older students to plan and write English essays.

The chapters follow a sequence for delivering the material. I applied these strategies with students in a clinical setting, then students took what they'd learned to their classroom and home to complete their schoolwork, but some of the basic strategies can be delivered to whole classes. For students requiring more intensive and targeted support, particular schemas and strategies can be applied to small groups. For students requiring more tailored supports, there are specific strategies that tutors and speech pathologists can apply to support students with vocabulary, sentence construction, paragraph composition, analysing texts and other areas.

This is not a resource on general instructional practices in the classroom but a book for professionals to support adolescent students with language and learning difficulties to complete essential writing tasks. Although you will notice that I have made some suggestions throughout the chapters for ways to introduce tasks to a whole class, the strategies are aimed at struggling students.

About Adolescents With Language and Learning Difficulties

Adolescence

There are many definitions of Adolescence. I thought it would be helpful to establish what I mean when using the terms adolescents and adolescence. The

World Health Organization refers to adolescence as 'the phase of life between childhood and adulthood, from ages 10 to 19,' which is a period of 'rapid physical, cognitive and psychosocial growth' (World Health Organization, 2021). Most researchers and clinicians subscribe to this definition, and this is the one I adhere to in this text when referring to adolescents and the period of adolescence.

The other reason for adopting this definition is so I can discuss these students within the specific context of academic settings and define the scope of the text. The scope extends to supporting students aged 10–19 with analysing written material to plan and write an English essay in class and during exams. I see the necessity for a range of language supports for adolescents who struggle, but I'm not proposing a one-stop shop. My aim is to propose a procedure for completing a specific task, the English essay, so it's necessary I constrain the boundaries to achieve this purpose.

The bulk of students in this age range will be attending high school, however either end of this age spectrum are students in upper primary and students in their first years of tertiary studies. The strategies offered are suitable for these students too. In fact, if students and teachers are familiar with the terminology and the processes inherent in the procedures for writing essays, this will ease transition between primary, secondary and tertiary classrooms. This way students have familiar, relevant tools that travel with them to their new settings.

Adolescent Performance: An Australian Perspective

In Australia, a Senate inquiry into the prevalence of communication disorders reported data on referrals made by General Practitioners. It reported the number of individuals who claimed for speech pathology services, under Medicare, from 2009–2014: There were 190,000 Medicare referrals for 0 to 4-year-olds, 280,000 referrals for 5 to 14-year-olds, then there was a radical decline in referrals for 15 to 24-year-olds, with less than 10,000 claiming for speech pathology services (Community Affairs References Committee, 2014).

In her submission to the senate inquiry, Professor Sharynne McLeod presented findings on the prevalence of learning difficulties in Australian schools. She reported that 36% of students in their first years of schooling presented with learning needs, which included up to 13% with communication disorder (Community Affairs References Committee, 2014).

According to research by McLeod and McKinnon (2007), up to 15% of students in their first year of schooling present with specific learning difficulties, while up to 16% of grade 10 students (15–16 years of age) presented with the same profile. Up to 14% of students in grade 11, and up to 12% of students in grade 12, presented with specific learning difficulties. Although there is a decline in numbers in later grades, McLeod and McKinnon hypothesise that students who have learning difficulties, and associated disorders, are more likely to exit the educational system early.

For those unfamiliar with the Australian education system, NAPLAN tests are administered each year in schools nation-wide. The purpose of testing is to gain insights into student ability. The results also compare the performance of students and schools. The NAPLAN data reports student results in a range of specific skill-related domains: Reading, Writing, Spelling, Grammar and Punctuation, and Numeracy. Tests are administered in grades 3, 5, 7 and 9. In 2021, 1.2 million students from over 9,000 schools participated (Australian Curriculum Assessment and Reporting Authority, 2021).

The NAPLAN website has several tables which compare results between 2008 and 2021 (Australian Curriculum Assessment and Reporting Authority, 2021).The comparisons are also made for domains (reading, writing etc.). Published results are both state-specific and Australia-wide. They report what percentage of students are performing below, at or above the minimum standard. The following information is from the preliminary statistics reported for Australia-wide results only, unless otherwise stated. The final results will be published in the NAPLAN National Report.

For Grade 3 students across Australia, the 2021 results indicate that achievement in Reading, Spelling, and Grammar and Punctuation was above when comparing to student performance in 2008. Writing and Numeracy achievement between 2008 and 2021 was not significantly different. Results indicate that students in Grade 5 made gains in Reading, Spelling, and Numeracy between 2008 and 2021.

For Grade 7 students in all domains, 2021 results showed achievement was not considered statistically higher than the base year 2008. Grade 9 results also show no significant losses or gains between 2008 and 2021.

NAPLAN also report preliminary data for students performing below the National Minimum Standard in 2021. The Grade 3 results show that the domain with the most students below minimum standard is Spelling, at 5.6%. In Grade 5, 5.3% of students performed below minimum standard in the Writing domain.

With 8.8% of students below minimum standard, Writing also proved to be the biggest challenge for struggling students in Grade 7. Not far behind, Grammar and Punctuation results placed 8.2% of Grade 7 students below minimum standard. In Grade 9, the preliminary results indicate that 16.2% of students performed below minimum standard for Writing.

For each grade, I have reported the domains with the most students below minimum standard, and as we can see, from Grade 5 onwards, writing appears to be the greatest challenge for adolescent students. And the data indicates that writing becomes more challenging as students get older.

So far, the data we have on school-age children suggests a gap between the high prevalence of language disorder in adolescents and low general practitioner referral rates to speech pathologists. NAPLAN data indicates that older students are continuing to struggle, which also suggests that while students who are underperforming might not be accessing speech pathology services, they're still struggling to be identified and receive appropriate support through schools.

And why are students still slipping in writing? It could be due to lack of teacher awareness on how to support older students with reading and writing difficulties, or even how to identify them. It could be a lack of targeted resources and strategies, time demands, staffing. And there will always be students who struggle with language and learning difficulties.

What we can see is that older students require assistance in our classrooms with text construction and written expression among other areas. If we are going to lift their performance, we should be able to identify these students in our high school classrooms and apply strategies to support them.

Characteristics of Language and Learning Difficulties in Adolescents

Students at this developmental stage are often acutely aware they have difficulties, and this makes them particularly sensitive about accessing therapy services and seeking help. There is evidence that adolescents treated for developmental language disorder experience low self-esteem, and that this continues beyond high school (Simkin & Conti-Ramsden, 2009). They are also at greater risk for school exclusion (Clegg et al., 2009).

In one study, the narrative skills of students in specialist behavioural school settings was found to be significantly poorer than their mainstream peers (James et al., 2020). Adolescent students with learning disabilities write less than typically developing peers and take more time to do so. They produce significantly poorer written texts as well as conversational texts (Bishop & Clarkson, 2003; Dockrell et al., 2009). They have poor knowledge of the structures of written texts and of the process for writing them, and have a poor understanding of text components, like the structure of a paragraph (Wong, 1997). Difficulties with writing expository texts will often persist beyond school if not addressed (Gregg et al., 2002). Inferencing is also difficult for adolescents with developmental language disorder (Karasinski & Ellis Weismer, 2010).

Adolescents with language difficulties avoid syntactic complexity and present with significantly poorer expressive skills than typically developing peers (Helland et al., 2014; Nippold et al., 2009; Tuller et al., 2012). They present with vocabulary deficits, but generally produce more nouns than verbs (Oetting et al., 1995; Windfuhr et al., 2002). Mackie and Dockrell (2004) observed that adolescents with language difficulties also write fewer words and produce more syntactic errors than typically developing peers.

Persistent language disorder has also been linked to increased risk for reading difficulties in later school years (Catts et al., 2002). In a systematic review, Anderson et al. (2016) found high incidences of language impairment in youth offenders; studies varied, from 25% to 87.5% of offenders testing in the clinical range for language disorder on standardised tests.

The research shows that language disorder doesn't disappear as children age. And there appears to be less awareness among teachers and other professionals on the presence of serious language deficits in the adolescent years and beyond. There is, however, a body of research supporting early intervention for language disorder and difficulties, but early learning and primary school teachers are still struggling to accurately identify and refer children who are at risk of falling behind with language and literacy (Antoniazzi et al., 2010; T. Christopulos & Kean, 2020).

Research on language disorder in adolescents is building each year, and what we do know is already very helpful. As we've seen, it tells us what to look for, areas to treat and how to approach this population.

Individuals who have developmental language disorder can present with a mild or more severe disorder. Some students will benefit from temporary, intensive supports, but there will be some students who will require constant support and accommodations with writing and language tasks. A longitudinal study showed that significant language difficulties in childhood can persist into adolescence and affect all areas of receptive and expressive language, both verbal and written (Stothard et al., 1998), so while putting our efforts into early intervention and robust response-to-intervention systems, we should be mindful there are students who will still struggle into high school and beyond.

Developmental language disorder is lifelong and it is estimated that roughly two students in every classroom have a developmental language disorder (Haddock & Walker, 2020; Norbury & Sonuga-Barke, 2017). Early intervention is crucial but, while we're working on this, we can still support older students.

Supporting Adolescents with Language and Learning Difficulties

For middle-school-aged students, scaffolding activities in a science classroom improved receptive but not expressive language in struggling students (Matson & Cline, 2012). Visual scaffolding that represented the role of word classes in sentences was found to significantly improve the sentence structure skills of adolescent students (Ebbels et al., 2014).

According to Dexter and Hughes (2011) who conducted a meta-analysis of available studies, "the use of graphic organizers was associated with increases in vocabulary knowledge, comprehension, and inferential knowledge," in older students with learning disabilities. More recently, Peterson et al. (2020) conducted a systematic review of the literature on the effectiveness of discourse intervention and found that interventions which provided explicit instructions, visual supports and student-made learning materials, like notes and use of graphic organisers, were the most effective strategies. Research also shows graphic organisers improve understanding of complicated tasks (Santangelo et al., 2007).

Content instruction is the domain of the teacher and tutor, while language support is concerned with facilitating the *processes* that students need to master, so they can access and learn the content (Larson & McKinley, 2003). But teachers can do both if they are supported. Making modifications to instructional language in classrooms can assist teachers to support students who are struggling, and there is evidence that teachers can continue to modify this independently after receiving assistance (Ehren, 2009; Starling et al., 2012).

In a meta-analysis of the literature on writing instruction for adolescent students, activities that provided specific strategies to structure students' persuasive and narrative texts proved to be the most effective treatments of all the instructions reviewed (Graham & Perin, 2007).

The research shows that graphic organisers and teaching the structure and function of texts and textual components are effective practices for supporting adolescents with language and learning difficulties. According to the literature, the visual representation of language structures improved understanding and output for struggling students. So, it appears that providing visual scaffolds and organisers for even one task and its associated processes will support improvement and have the greatest overall impact for older students struggling with language and learning.

Memory, Processing and Schemas

We've learned a bit about how adolescents with language and learning difficulties can present, and what types of approaches work for this cohort. This section offers some basic information on typical memory and thinking processes. It surveys the relevance of these cognitive functions, their interdependence on each other and the ways in which they are thought to underpin language and learning.

If you are a teacher and have students in your class with language and learning difficulties—and statistically, you most likely do—you will also read reports and attend meetings where you will encounter discussions on memory and processing, so understanding these topics will prove useful for you and your students.

Schemas and Scaffolds

Our brains have schemas for just about everything. They are mental representations that allow us to understand the world. A semantic schema for 'cat,' for example, would contain all the facts we know about cats: animal, small, four legs, fury, pet, purrs, jumps high and so on, enough information for us to be able to know what someone is referring to when they mention cats. Even abstract concepts and themes can be said to have schemas (Davis et al., 2020).

We have schemas for social situations so we know how to behave and what is expected, although these schemas are more fluid, and may differ slightly, or a lot, between individuals depending on our specific experiences. For example, we all have a schema for a doctor's appointment; because when a doctor asks *how are you?* your response will not be the same one you'd give to a stranger asking that same question. And schemas are how we know this without having to think consciously about it and embarrass ourselves.

We subconsciously draw on many schemas about what things are, how they work and why, so we can understand the world and interact with it in a way that is shared by those around us—imagine having to be told what a dog is every time you encounter one. In the same way, imagine having to re-learn the basic structure of a story every time you watch a movie, or re-learn the structure of a letter every time you write one. If you encounter a problem or need to analyse a situation, you subconsciously draw on your internal schemas to make sense of the world and interact with it.

Scaffolds are different but can complement schemas. If you're not familiar with the concept, think of learning scaffolds like scaffolding in a building; on a building site, they assist workers to form the main structure and once the structure is complete, the scaffolds come down. Scaffolds to support learning include anything provided to help complete a task. Once the task is complete, the scaffolds come down and what remains is an improved understanding or finished product. Graphic organisers and picture sequences are some examples of scaffolding strategies. Of course, some students might always need particular scaffolds, and certain types of accommodations to support their understanding and expression.

You can read more on the nature and function of schemas at the end of this section where I outline research on schemas and discourse.

About Memory

There are two basic types of memory systems: declarative and non-declarative. You might also find them referred to as explicit and implicit memory respectively.

Declarative memory is about what you know, the content. This is where vocabulary and word meaning live. Having just read about schemas, you might make the link between a schema for knowing what a cat is, and declarative memory, and if not, now you have. This is semantic memory, what we traditionally think of as knowledge. It's what we know about the world, the objects in it and how they interact. Memory for recalling events, what happened to you and when, is also part of declarative memory. This is called episodic memory. Declarative memories are consciously accessed for the most part.

Procedural memory is non-declarative memory. This is memory for processes and is subconsciously activated. It is associated with learning new skills, and for improving and honing existing ones. It's about *how* we do things. Storing memories as procedures saves time. It's the reason we do not need to memorise how to open every single door we encounter; even though handles, doors and buildings all look different, we can transfer the procedure of 'door opening' to any context that presents us with all the features in our schema for 'doors' and how they work.

Examples of procedural memory activation also include buttoning your shirt, using a knife and fork, and includes formulating sentences using syntax (again we do not apply syntax consciously when we speak). Procedural memory helps us adhere to narrative structure to tell a story. When someone asks *how was your day?* You can answer by recalling what you did (declarative memory), and telling them in an ordered way that follows a pattern, starting with where you were, when it happened, who was there and the order of events which all follow a subconscious, mental procedure for applying narrative structure. And when your doctor asks *What can I do for you?* you will trigger a shorter version of this narrative procedure to retell a story about where you were, when the pain started and so on.

To store and retrieve memories for objects, episodes and procedures is thought to require schemas. When people refer to having something to hang your hat on, schemas are where the hats hang.

When we encounter new information, schemas make it easier, and more efficient, to process, to problem solve and to retain new information. This area where new and existing information meet is called working memory. If our schemas are poorly formed, then our minds work so much harder to process and retain information. Since our working memory capacity is limited, automatic processes ensure we don't congest our limited capacity. Automaticity means we make the most with the room we have to problem solve.

Thinking Processes

There are two types of problem-solving processes that I'd like to discuss because I think they are relevant for the purposes of this book. These are heuristic models and reflective models.

Heuristic processing is the path of least resistance, it's the snap decision based on simple and immediate observations. Using this type of processing, you can decide that someone is right because they are an expert, or agree with a plan because the majority does (Chaiken, 1980). Another example would be thinking someone is a good or bad person depending on their gender or wardrobe choice, which is an unhelpful and unfair way to process the world. But this type of processing has its advantages when applied appropriately. For example, heuristic processing means that you will take the medications your doctor prescribes without feeling compelled to carry out extensive research or complete a pharmaceutical degree to establish if the prescription is appropriate. Heuristics can also help us estimate the amount of time we will put aside to complete a task. They can also help us associate certain qualities and characteristics with certain themes. The idea is that these mental short-cuts can enhance recall and save valuable processing time.

Reflective or systematic processing is what we do when we analyse information before we draw conclusions or act. This involves thinking about what we know and applying it to what we see, asking questions and making decisions based on the logic we can draw out of a scenario. We evaluate on a case-by-case basis when we process information reflectively (or systematically). We question consciously, accessing our declarative (semantic and episodic) and non-declarative (procedural) knowledge about the world (Chen et al., 1999). We will also look for external information to make decisions, by reading books, articles and searching the internet.

Both represent ways of processing that are mediated by schemas. Heuristic processes are about stereotypes and guesswork based on previous knowledge or experience and are quite narrow and easy to access. Reflective processing is harder to access and involves questioning and evaluating a situation to see how it might fit with or deviate from existing patterns and knowledge.

Typically developing language and cognitive faculties support individuals to develop age-appropriate schematic knowledge and processing skills. And now we might be able to see how students with memory and attention difficulties, for example, might struggle to build schemas, and do the processing necessary for evaluating the world and the events and objects within it.

As we have seen from the evidence on effective strategies for adolescents with language and learning difficulties, there are ways we can scaffold language and make accommodations to support students with poorer memory and attention, and learning difficulties. And we can support students to apply different types of thinking processes by providing scaffolded activities which assist students to apply problem-solving strategies to academic tasks, strategies that support students to reflect and evaluate.

Schema and Discourse Research and Language and Learning Difficulties

The following is a sample of research on schemas and how we use them. Some of the studies describe theories and research based on the performance of students with disabilities, while some are studies of cohorts comprised of typically developing subjects.

By establishing what is thought to typically occur when adolescents process texts, and how schemas are thought to mediate this process, we might develop a clearer understanding of what could be missing for students who struggle with these mental structures and processes. We can also see how researchers have put the theory, and definitions of schemas, memory and thinking processes into practice to determine what structures and systems support text comprehension and construction.

We know that when schemas are learned and automatic, they are helpful knowledge structures that place less demand on working memory, allowing more time to process new information (Long & Lea, 2005), but schemas can be useful even if they are not overlearned and internalised.

Schema theory has been applied to assist students who struggle with mathematics (Marshall, 1995). There are studies on the use of schema-based instruction to support word-based problem solving in mathematics, where visual organisers (elements like pictures and diagrams) represent the problem types, and students are taught when and how to apply the relevant schema (Peltier et al., 2021; Powell, 2011; Root et al., 2017).

Patterns in texts can also help support retention and recall of information. Repeated syntactic patterns like "what do you hear?" from a picture book, create schematic frames which attempt to make information more memorable for students (Zipprich et al., 2009). The idea being that frames support long-term retention and retrieval.

Reading and comprehension are supported by both knowledge of a text and background knowledge (Kamil, 2002), and on reviewing available studies,

Brewer and Nakamura (1984) established schemas play a crucial role in comprehension and recall, even when a title or picture was supplied just before subjects read. Visual schemas for text-structures provide a framework for comprehension, functioning as a type of template where readers (and listeners) can insert information.

Narratives are situational and sequential, but this does not mean that narratives are only understood when presented as such. In a study where students were presented with a range of narratives, some with events out of order, students still showed a preference for recalling the stories by retelling the events as they occurred over time rather than where they were presented in the original narrative (Bower et al., 1979), which demonstrates the role of schemas in assisting our understanding, retention and expression.

Learning narrative schemas early may well lay the groundwork for developing more advanced comprehension later, with these early—but vital—schemas becoming automatic and passive vessels for comprehending actions and events, freeing up room in working memory so conscious processes can do more advanced evaluation. It seems that learning narrative schemas at a young age pays dividends later. Understanding how narrative texts are organised appears to improve retention and recall of narrative content. But is there a difference between schemas for narrative and expository discourse?

Research shows that students' recall of expository text was more successful where the texts included mainly cause-effect content, whereas expository texts containing compare-and-contrast content were not summarised as successfully (Lundine et al., 2018).

Larson and McKinley (2003) documented the key differences between narrative and expository texts and found, among other things, that narrative texts can be interpreted through pragmatic and experiential inferencing, while expository texts rely on logical-deductive thinking to be fully understood. Berman and Nir-Sagiv (2007) found that expository schemas, unlike narrative, were more category-based.

Narrative texts tend to follow a more concrete sequence of events and contain cause and effect content. Studies show students master narrative texts before expository text-types (Berman & Nir-Sagiv, 2007). Expository texts will contain more advanced grammar and vocabulary and require more global coherence, and so are not generally mastered, or taught, until adolescence (Berman & Nir-Sagiv, 2007; Larson & McKinley, 2003; Paul, 2001). And this makes sense because perspective-taking, which assists students to argue and persuade, is thought to develop from 7–9 years of age (Paul, 2001).

Theories and research on the cognitive processes that support comprehending texts propose that certain processes support situational understanding of texts; understanding and retention of things like actions, events, their chronology, how characters are connected, consequences and so on. These processes are considered passive, they are thought to happen automatically in typical readers. Then there's reader-initiated processes. These can include any number of conscious actions on the part of the reader, ranging from re-reading a sentence, and notetaking, to interpreting texts (Van den Broek & Helder, 2017). Reader-initiated processes are effortful; this means the reader is consciously applying techniques to understand a text. Reader-initiated processes can help with repairs, when meaning breaks down, but they are also thought to underpin more advanced evaluation of texts. Van den Broek and Helder (2017) posit that reader-initiated processes work in tandem with passive processes to aid text comprehension, and that this creates greater coherence and more in-depth understanding of texts.

According to research, schemas support retaining and recalling situational information, but this is not all we do with information. There's more still to be gleaned from schema research on the type of processing required for analysing texts.

Bransford and Johnson (1972) established the role of topics in activating information to support comprehension, which has been replicated in research since (Brewer & Nakamura, 1984; Smith & Swinney, 1992). Global coherence, which research suggests is reader-initiated, requires us to connect new information we read or hear with themes and topics (Long & Lea, 2005), which leads to a richer understanding of texts.

There is alignment between schema research on understanding discourse (narrative and expository texts), the requirements of typical memory and processing, and strategies that the literature recommends for supporting adolescents with language and learning difficulties. For example, there's efficacy for applying graphic organisers to arrange and classify information, like mind-mapping and box-arrow models, which are visual representations of the type of semantic networking facilitated by schemas. There's efficacy for using visual scaffolds to support sentence formulation, and the literature describes the use of visual representations to mediate text understanding and construction. Schema and discourse research outlines the type of processing we want to see happen, how this typically happens and suggests the type of supports we can offer students when these mental processes breakdown.

So, What Now?

The literature indicates that if struggling students are to formulate stronger mental representations from reading and listening to narrative and expository information, then they will benefit from topic-guided schemas that support explicit and reader-initiated processes to mediate and improve understanding. It also seems that, to be successful, these schemas ought to be highly visual—in the form of graphic organisers and visual scaffolds—to support both comprehension and expression at sentence, paragraph and text levels.

This book represents a practical, sequenced and task-focused application of writing strategies. It offers schemas to support constructing an expository text, but also schemas to support text analysis and idea synthesis in a way that leads with themes, their identification and relevance to the text. The schemas and strategies are graphic representations of the language and thinking processes which I have identified as relevant for secondary students I've worked with. I've applied and shaped them in the clinic since I started in private practice and have seen them work time and time again, lifting the performance of many students.

The strategies support the English essay writing task, so students can access, and express, deeper understanding of texts. The process is explained so that teachers and other professionals can support students to learn and apply these tools. Empowered with these strategies, students can then write their own notes as they go, building their notes into sentences, sentences into paragraphs, and paragraphs into fully formed texts, eventually writing their own English essays.

References

Anderson, S. A. S., Hawes, D. J., & Snow, P. C. (2016). Language impairments among youth offenders: A systematic review. *Children and Youth Services Review, 65*, 195–203. https://doi.org/10.1016/j.childyouth.2016.04.004

Antoniazzi, D., Snow, P., & Dickson-Swift, V. (2010). Teacher identification of children at risk for language impairment in the first year of school. *International Journal of Speech Language Pathology, 12*(3), 244–252. https://doi.org/10.3109/17549500903104447

Australian Curriculum Assessment and Reporting Authority. (2021). *Preliminary results.* ACARA. Retrieved October 7, 2021, from https://reports.acara.edu.au/NAP/NaplanResults

Berman, R. A., & Nir-Sagiv, B. (2007). Comparing narrative and expository text construction across adolescence: A developmental paradox. *Discourse Processes, 43*(2), 79–120. https://doi.org/10.1207/s15326950dp4302_1

Bishop, D. V. M., & Clarkson, B. (2003). Written language as a window into residual language deficits: A study of children with persistent and residual speech and language impairments. *Cortex, 39*(2), 215–237.

Bower, G. H., Black, J. B., & Turner, T. J. (1979). Scripts in memory for text. *Cognitive Psychology, 11*(2), 177–220. https://doi.org/10.1016/0010-0285(79)90009-4

Bransford, J. D., & Johnson, M. K. (1972). Contextual prerequisites for understanding: Some investigations of comprehension and recall. *Journal of Verbal Learning and Verbal Behavior, 11*(6), 717–726. https://doi.org/10.1016/S0022-5371(72)80006-9

Brewer, W. F., & Nakamura, G. V. (1984). The nature and functions of schemas. In *Handbook of social cognition* (Vol. 1, pp. 118–160). Lawrence Erlbaum Associates Publishers.

Catts, H. W., Fey, M. E., Tomblin, J. B., & Zhang, X. (2002). A longitudinal investigation of reading outcomes in children with language impairments. *Journal of Speech, Language, and Hearing Research, 45*(6), 1142–1157. https://doi.org/10.1044/1092-4388(2002/093)

Chaiken, S. (1980). Heuristic versus systematic information processing and the use of source versus message cues in persuasion. *Journal of Personality and Social Psychology, 39*(5), 752–766. https://doi.org/10.1037/0022-3514.39.5.752

Chen, S., Duckworth, K., & Chaiken, S. (1999). Motivated heuristic and systematic processing. *Psychological Inquiry, 10*(1), 44–49. https://doi.org/10.1207/s15327965pli1001_6

Christopulos, T. T., & Kean, J. (2020). General education teachers' contribution to the identification of children with language disorders. *Perspectives of the ASHA Special Interest Groups, 5*(4), 770–777. https://doi.org/10.1044/2020_PERSP-19-00166

Clegg, J., Stackhouse, J., Finch, K., Murphy, C., & Nicholls, S. (2009). Language abilities of secondary age pupils at risk of school exclusion: A preliminary report. *Child Language Teaching and Therapy, 25*(1), 123–139. https://doi.org/10.1177/0265659008098664

Community Affairs References Committee. (2014). *Prevalence of different types of speech, language and communication disorders and speech pathology services in Australia.* Commonwealth of Australia.

Davis, C. P., Altmann, G. T. M., & Yee, E. (2020). Situational systematicity: A role for schema in understanding the differences between abstract and concrete concepts. *Cognitive Neuropsychology, 37*(1–2), 142–153. https://doi.org/10.1080/02643294.2019.1710124

Dexter, D. D., & Hughes, C. A. (2011). Graphic organizers and students with learning disabilities: A meta-analysis. *Learning Disability Quarterly, 34*(1), 51–72. https://doi.org/10.1177/073194871103400104

Dockrell, J. E., Lindsay, G., & Connelly, V. (2009). The impact of specific language impairment on adolescents' written text. *Exceptional Children, 75*(4), 427–446. https://doi.org/10.1177/001440290907500403

Ebbels, S. H., Marić, N., Murphy, A., & Turner, G. (2014). Improving comprehension in adolescents with severe receptive language impairments: A randomized control trial of intervention for coordinating conjunctions: Improving comprehension in adolescents with severe receptive language impairments. *International Journal of Language & Communication Disorders, 49*(1), 30–48. https://doi.org/10.1111/1460-6984.12047

Ehren, B. J. (2009). Response-to-intervention: SLPs as linchpins in secondary schools. *ASHA Leader, 14*(6), 10–13. https://doi.org/10.1044/leader.FTR1.14062009.10

Graham, S., & Perin, D. (2007). A meta-analysis of writing instruction for adolescent students. *Journal of Educational Psychology, 99*(3), 445–476. https://doi.org/10.1037/0022-0663.99.3.445

Gregg, N., Coleman, C., Stennett, R. B., & Davis, M. (2002). Discourse complexity of college writers with and without disabilities: A multidimensional analysis. *Journal of Learning Disabilities, 35*(1), 23–38. https://doi.org/10.1177/002221940203500103

Haddock, R., & Walker, C. (2020). *Developmental language disorder: A disability, health and education challenge* (p. 20). A. H. A. H. Association.

Helland, W. A., Helland, T., & Heimann, M. (2014). Language profiles and mental health problems in children with specific language impairment and children with ADHD. *Journal of Attention Disorders, 18*(3), 226–235. https://doi.org/10.1177/1087054712441705

James, K., Munro, N., Togher, L., & Cordier, R. (2020). The spoken language and social communication characteristics of adolescents in behavioral schools: A controlled comparison study. *Language, Speech & Hearing Services in Schools, 51*(1), 115–127. https://doi.org/10.1044/2019_LSHSS-18-0090

Kamil, M. L. (2002). *Methods of literacy research: The methodology chapters from the handbook of reading research* (Vol. III). L. Erlbaum Associates. https://doi.org/10.4324/9781410604460

Karasinski, C., & Ellis Weismer, S. (2010). Comprehension of inferences in discourse processing by adolescents with and without language impairment. *Journal of Speech, Language, and Hearing Research, 53*(5), 1268–1279. https://doi.org/10.1044/1092-4388(2009/09-0006)

Larson, V. L., & McKinley, N. L. (2003). *Communication solutions for older students: Assessment and intervention strategies.* Thinking Pub.

Long, D. L., & Lea, R. B. (2005). Have we been searching for meaning in all the wrong places? Defining the "search after meaning" principle in comprehension. *Discourse Processes, 39*(2–3), 279–298. https://doi.org/10.1080/0163853X.2005.9651684

Lundine, J. P., Harnish, S. M., McCauley, R. J., Blackett, D. S., Zezinka, A., Chen, W., & Fox, R. A. (2018). Adolescent summaries of narrative and expository discourse: Differences and predictors. *Language, Speech & Hearing Services in Schools, 49*(3), 551–568. https://doi.org/10.1044/2018_LSHSS-17-0105

Mackie, C., & Dockrell, J. E. (2004). The nature of written language deficits in children with SLI. *Journal of Speech, Language, and Hearing Research*, *47*(6), 1469–1483. https://doi.org/10.1044/1092-4388(2004/109)

Marshall, S. P. (1995). *Schemas in problem solving*. Cambridge University Press.

Matson, G., & Cline, T. (2012). The impact of specific language impairment on performance in science and suggested implications for pedagogy. *Child Language Teaching and Therapy*, *28*(1), 25–37. https://doi.org/10.1177/0265659011414276

McLeod, S., & McKinnon, D. H. (2007). Prevalence of communication disorders compared with other learning needs in 14 500 primary and secondary school students. *International Journal of Language & Communication Disorders*, *42*(S1), 37–59. https://doi.org/10.1080/13682820601173262

Nippold, M. A., Mansfield, T. C., Billow, J. L., & Tomblin, J. B. (2009). Syntactic development in adolescents with a history of language impairments: A follow-up investigation. *American Journal of Speech-Language Pathology*, *18*(3), 241–251. https://doi.org/10.1044/1058-0360(2008/08-0022)

Norbury, C. F., & Sonuga-Barke, E. (2017). Editorial: New frontiers in the scientific study of developmental language disorders. *Journal of Child Psychology and Psychiatry*, *58*(10), 1065–1067. https://doi.org/10.1111/jcpp.12821

Oetting, J. B., Rice, M. L., & Swank, L. K. (1995). Quick incidental learning (QUIL) of words by school-age children with and without SLI. *Journal of Speech and Hearing Research*, *38*(2), 434–445. https://doi.org/10.1044/jshr.3802.434

Paul, R. (2001). *Language disorders from infancy through adolescence: Assessment & intervention* (2nd ed.). Mosby.

Peltier, C., Lingo, M. E., Autry, F., Deardorff, M. E., & Palacios, M. (2021). Schema-based instruction implemented under routine conditions. *Journal of Applied School Psychology*, *37*(3), 246–267. https://doi.org/10.1080/15377903.2020.1821273

Peterson, A. K., Fox, C. B., & Israelsen, M. (2020). A systematic review of academic discourse interventions for school-aged children with language-related learning disabilities. *Language, Speech & Hearing Services in Schools*, *51*(3), 866–881. https://doi.org/10.1044/2020_LSHSS-19-00039

Powell, S. R. (2011). Solving word problems using schemas: A review of the literature. *Learning Disabilities Research and Practice*, *26*(2), 94–108. https://doi.org/10.1111/j.1540-5826.2011.00329.x

Root, J. R., Browder, D. M., Saunders, A. F., & Lo, Y. (2017). Schema-based instruction with concrete and virtual manipulatives to teach problem solving to students with autism. *Remedial and Special Education*, *38*(1), 42–52. https://doi.org/10.1177/0741932516643592

Santangelo, T. H., Karen, R., & Graham, S. (2007). Self-regulated strategy development: A validated model to support students who struggle with writing. *Learning Disabilities: A Contemporary Journal*, *5*(1), 1–20.

Simkin, Z., & Conti-Ramsden, G. (2009). I went to a language unit': Adolescents' views on specialist educational provision and their language difficulties. *Child Language Teaching and Therapy*, *25*(1), 103–121. https://doi.org/10.1177/0265659008098663

Smith, E. E., & Swinney, D. A. (1992). The role of schemas in reading text: A real-time examination. *Discourse Processes*, *15*(3), 303–316. https://doi.org/10.1080/01638539209544814

Starling, J., Munro, N., Togher, L., & Arciuli, J. (2012). Training secondary school teachers in instructional language modification techniques to support adolescents with language impairment: A randomized controlled trial. *Language, Speech & Hearing Services in Schools*, *43*(4), 474–495. https://doi.org/10.1044/0161-1461(2012/11-0066)

Stothard, S. E., Snowling, M. J., Bishop, D. V. M., Chipchase, B. B., & Kaplan, C. A. (1998). Language-impaired preschoolers: A follow-up into adolescence. *Journal of Speech, Language, and Hearing Research*, *41*(2), 407–418. https://doi.org/10.1044/jslhr.4102.407

Tuller, L., Henry, C., Sizaret, E. V. A., & Barthez, M.-A. (2012). Specific language impairment at adolescence: Avoiding complexity. *Applied Psycholinguistics*, *33*(1), 161–184. https://doi.org/10.1017/S0142716411000312

Van den Broek, P., & Helder, A. (2017). Cognitive processes in discourse comprehension: Passive processes, reader-initiated processes, and evolving mental representations. *Discourse Processes*, *54*(5–6), 360–372. https://doi.org/10.1080/0163853X.2017.1306677

Windfuhr, K. L., Faragher, B., & Conti-Ramsden, G. (2002). Lexical learning skills in young children with specific language impairment (SLI). *International Journal of Language & Communication Disorders*, *37*(4), 415–432. https://doi.org/10.1080/1368282021000007758

Wong, B. Y. L. (1997). Research on genre-specific strategies for enhancing writing in adolescents with learning disabilities. *Learning Disability Quarterly*, *20*(2), 140–159. https://doi.org/10.2307/1511220

World Health Organization. (2021). *Adolescent health*. World Health Organization. Retrieved September 30, 2021, from https://www.who.int/health-topics/adolescent-health#tab=tab_1

Zipprich, M. A., Grace, M., & Grote-Garcia, S. A. (2009). Building story schema: Using patterned books as a means of instruction for students with disabilities. *Intervention in School and Clinic*, *44*(5), 294–299. https://doi.org/10.1177/1053451208330896

1 A Way to Analyse Texts

> Did You Know...
> Numerous studies show that graphic organisers aid comprehension, vocabulary and inferencing skills (Dexter & Hughes, 2011). In one study, students' text comprehension improved when they applied a scaffold to what they read. The scaffold helped them link ideas and knowledge rather than simply memorising details in texts (Alvermann, 1981). Swanson (1999) looked at different types of instruction given to students with learning disabilities in the classroom and found that learning improved when students were prompted to apply strategies, and when tasks were sequenced, made visual, scaffolded and included steps for problem solving.

Students require ways into texts that go beyond retelling. One of the biggest concerns I hear from English teachers is that struggling students will often refer to characters and events in a text without making evaluative comments or discussing texts with greater depth. While analysis isn't a requirement for younger students, it is expected that adolescents, especially in secondary schools, will be able to interpret texts and demonstrate greater depth of understanding.

Recalling a story is important, and there are schemas that demonstrate the parts of a narrative and that include narrative macrostructures (character introduction, setting, character goal etc.) in sequence. You and your students can use these to capture elements of the story. Summarising the plot will support student understanding and serve as a quick reference to support recollection of narrative events.

I have included an example of a basic narrative schema in the Appendix, but an online search for narrative scaffolds or narrative planners will give you an idea of the types of freely available templates out there. Since this book is specifically for English essay text analysis and writing, I will not go into any great depth on narrative schema.

DOI: 10.4324/9781003263401-2

Identifying Themes

Before we launch into text analysis, we might need to address vocabulary.

Essential terms can be easily overlooked, especially if there is a lot of content to be covered in a short time. And sometimes, certain terms are assumed knowledge. The following are some essential, basic terms students will need to understand to apply the schemas in the book. This isn't the only vocabulary students will need, and I will cover further terms when relevant.

> text-type
> genre
> theme

You might like to write the three terms across a board, or on a notepad if working one-to-one. Once you have defined each term, checked understanding, then provided some examples, students could work in pairs to list a few examples of their own, then you could populate the list by asking students to add their examples to a poster that you might keep on the wall—see figure 1.1 for an example list. Bear in mind that the lists, especially for text and theme, can get quite long. Virtually anything can be a theme, so long as it forms a noun (person, place, or thing).

It might also help at this point to think of some possible synonyms for 'theme,' like 'topic,' 'idea,' 'concept' or 'category.' This might help students understand that theme can be used interchangeably with these other terms, but all mean basically the same thing.

You might also take the opportunity to refine and reinforce the definitions, making them more memorable. Once you've completed your lists, review one list at a time and decide what the examples have in common. You might decide that a text-type can be made specifically to be viewed and consumed on some sort of intellectual or mental level. This is as true for a novel as much as it is for a sculpture, and delineates these two types from say a pen, or a stove, which are clearly not text-types. Doing this might support students to understand why some things, like a painting or sculpture, are text-types and why other types of objects are not referred to as such.

Text-types	Genres	Themes
novel	*action*	*belonging*
play	*comedy*	*identity*
feature film	*romance*	*beast within*
short film	*rom-com*	*nature*
sitcom	*sci-fi/*	*war*
editorial	*fantasy...*	*love*
a painting...		*death...*

Figure 1.1

A Way to Analyse Texts 19

For example definitions refer to the entry in the Appendix. You can use this as a type of 'cheat sheet.' I would encourage you to write down your final definitions, so you have an easy reference.

text-type:
genre:
theme:

For further reinforcement, students could draw rings (figure 1.2) in their notebooks, then transfer the words from the list into the correct areas. The rings are a visual representation of the somewhat hierarchical but interconnected relationship among the three terms.

It might be handy for students to know that when authors or artists decide to create something, they decide what text-type they will use, and perhaps decide

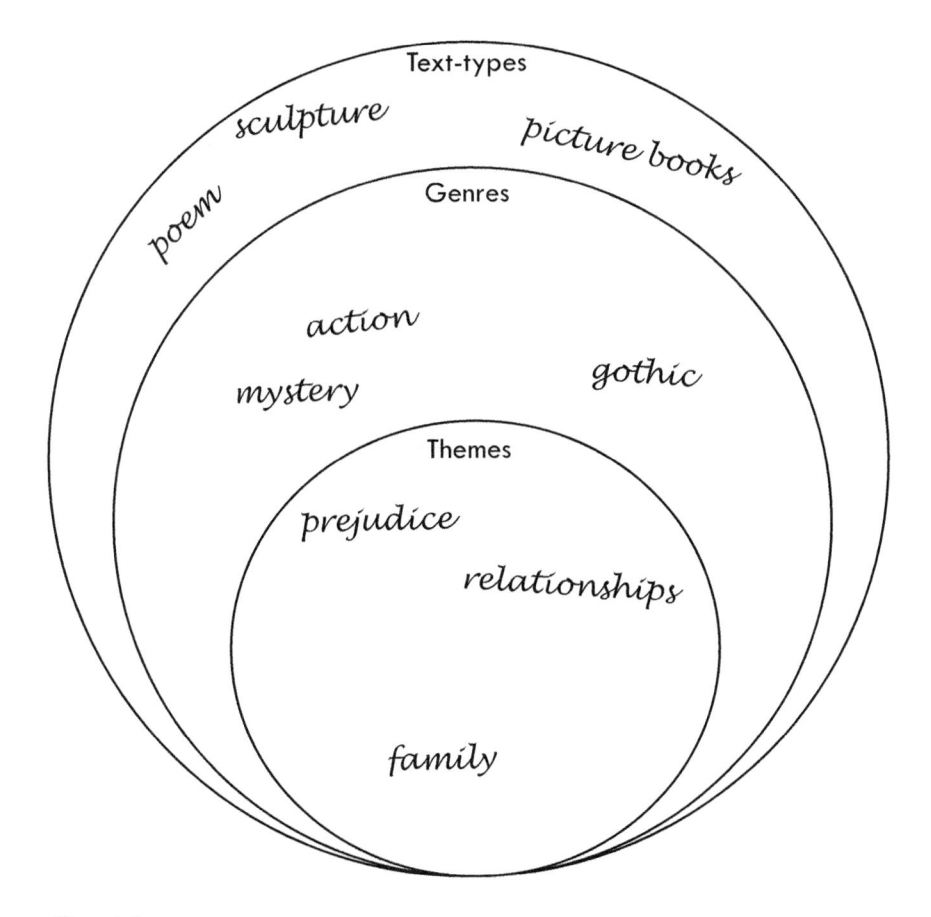

Figure 1.2

the genre and themes before they go about creating characters and plots. When they're finished, what they have is called a text. Of course, we know the work doesn't stop there as authors continue to shape and edit, but this is enough of an explanation for students to get the gist of the process.

Worksheet: Text, Theme, Genre

Collect 5 texts from anywhere: the living room, classroom, maybe the library. Use the information from your genre/text-type/theme scaffold on page 11, and write a sentence about all five texts. Use the scaffold below to help you shape your sentences.

Texts can fall into more than one genre, but try and stick to one. If you need to, look-up the elements for each genre.

At times, it may seem like this exercise is over-simplifying the texts, but remember this is a starting point for understanding what texts are, how vocabulary like genre and theme relate to each other, and to scaffold expression using clear grammar.

The _____, _____ by _____ is a _____ about _____.

      text-type   text (title)   creator   genre   theme

1 _____

2 _____

3 _____

4 _____

5 _____

Worksheet 1.1

Students might want to know that most texts have titles. Some texts specify the author or artists that produced them. Some have many names attached to them, for instance a TV episode of *The Big Bang Theory* is a text that is created by many people including a screenwriter, producers, directors and many more. *Romeo and Juliet* is also a text, more specifically, a play.

Worksheet 1.1 presents an opportunity for learning and writing practice at sentence level. So far, it might seem like we are oversimplifying the texts, but remember this is a starting point for understanding what texts are, how vocabulary like genre and theme relate to each other, and how to scaffold expression using clear grammar.

Now we have some terms defined, and we know what sorts of things can be classified as a theme, it's time students had a go at identifying them in a text. For this, they will use our first schema. We'll call it the Text + Theme schema, and we will use it for inferencing and evaluating. Students might want to know that inferencing is how we interpret a text and this might be the same or different from what an author intends. Since students can't know for sure what the author wants the reader to think, then all they can do is infer and interpret meaning from the text.

The schema introduced in the next section is a core component of the process outlined in this book, not only of our analysis, but for structuring and writing essays. It will be referred to throughout this text.

The Text + Theme Schema

In English class, students must demonstrate that they understand and can analyse texts. Most will understand the basic storyline, and others will need assistance to comprehend the storyline. Some might agree on some of the ideas in the text, but for others the details and ideas in the story might be understood differently; the text might imply one thing, while the reader or viewer of a text might infer their own ideas.

The schema in figure 1.3 is a core component, not only of our text analysis, but of the process for structuring and writing essays covered in this book. I will refer to it throughout, so it would be helpful for students to learn it well, or at least have a copy in the back of their notebooks for reference and application.

We won't address all the parts of this scaffold now. First, we will focus on theme. Time for a story!

I thought I'd choose an oldie but a goodie—*Little Red Riding Hood*. There are many versions and re-workings of the story, so this is one version. This fairy tale has gone under much analysis and interpretation, but here we'll keep it simple. This works for upper primary and secondary students alike.

> *Little Red Riding Hood*
> Once upon a time, in a little shack on the edge of a dark forest lived a little girl. One day she decided to visit her ailing grandmother. Grandma lived far away, and the only path was through the dark woods. The girl's father packed some food. Her mother gave her a red, hooded cape for the cold journey, then the little girl set off through the forest.

'Text + Theme'
Schema

Text   Theme

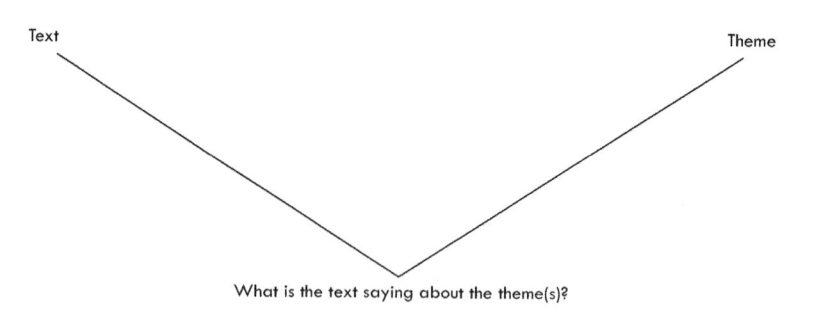

What is the text saying about the theme(s)?

Figure 1.3

After a time, she stopped to rest. As she sat, the bushes rustled. A wolf appeared, raised on his back legs. Startled, the little girl jumped, dropping her basket.

"Don't be afraid," said the wolf. "I won't harm you." The wolf looked at the basket. "What's in there?"

"None of your business," she replied, snatching up her basket.

The wolf frowned, "No need to be rude. I was just curious. These woods are lonely. I only meant to acquaint myself with you in the hope of some polite conversation, but never mind." The wolf turned to leave.

"Wait," said the little girl. "I don't mean to be impolite." The wolf turned and smiled. She continued, "I have food in the basket, for my grandma. She is old and ill and I am on my way to her now."

"Oh," said the wolf, "I'm sorry to hear your grandma is ill. Have you travelled far to see her?"

"Yes, but I still have a way to go, yet!"

"How far exactly?"

The little girl explained to the wolf exactly how far, and where, she had to go. The wolf shook his head. "That does sound like a long way. You'd best be off then. Thank you for the conversation." And with that, the little girl waved the wolf goodbye and continued her journey. "What a nice wolf," she thought.

When the little girl arrived at grandma's house, the door was already open. Fearing the worst, she rushed inside and to her relief, found grandma safely tucked into bed—but she looked different. "Grandma, what big eyes you have," said the little girl.

"All the better to see you with," replied grandma.

"And your ears are bigger too!"

"All the better to hear you with my darling."

The little girl gasped, "and how your teeth have grown!"

"All the better to eat you with," said grandma, only it wasn't grandma. The wolf sprung up from under the sheets and launched himself across the room.

After a time, the room fell silent. The wolf licked his paws then adjusted his bonnet. A loud burp escaped from his mouth. He patted his full belly. "Two big meals in one day," contemplated the wolf, "I'd best have some rest before I see what's on the menu tomorrow," and with that he lay down on the bed and thumbed the label on the red hooded cape. It said, 'If found please return to 25 Meadow Lane.' The wolf grinned a vicious grin.

In this version of the tale, the wolf wins. It was chosen because students are more likely to be familiar with the fairy tale thereby reducing, or in some cases eliminating, the need to break down and comprehend the text at this stage. This means that you can use this text, and other fairy tales and fables, to practise the Text + Theme schema. Once students learn how to apply the schema (and its variations) to familiar texts like this, then they can try applying the process to unfamiliar texts.

Let's start filling in our Text + Theme schema, using this version of *Little Red Riding Hood*. Once students have finished reading or you have read the story to them, you might start by writing the scaffold on the board (just two diagonal lines that meet underneath). Tutors or speech pathologists working one-to-one or in small groups, might write this on a note pad. You could also print and hand out the sheet presented in what follows. Students could glue a copy into the back of their notebooks.

We write the name of the text we are analysing on the left, then start listing themes on the right. When students start listing themes, it is important for them to understand that many topics can be themes in a text, so encourage students to list them all. You might like to add your own examples too: The little girl in the story is walking through the forest, so write 'nature,' she meets a strange wolf, so 'strangers.' She's wearing a red cape—it's in the title, so it might be important—so why not write 'fashion'?

What is important for students to realise is that even though some themes might seem weak and irrelevant, and some more important, and much stronger, we can cull the list later. Also, listing everything is a good motivator; it helps them all get started, and the struggling students get a win—it demonstrates they comprehend the exercise. Mind you, if someone names 'aviation' as a theme in *Little Red Riding Hood*, then they're probably a little off-track.

Students in class or small groups might start listing themes in pairs for 5 minutes. Encourage struggling students to choose words straight off the page. Once they have a few themes, then you can ask paired students to add them to the board.

Your board or notepad might look something like figure 1.4 as you start to develop the list of themes as a whole class, as small groups or with one student.

24   *A Way to Analyse Texts*

Text   Theme

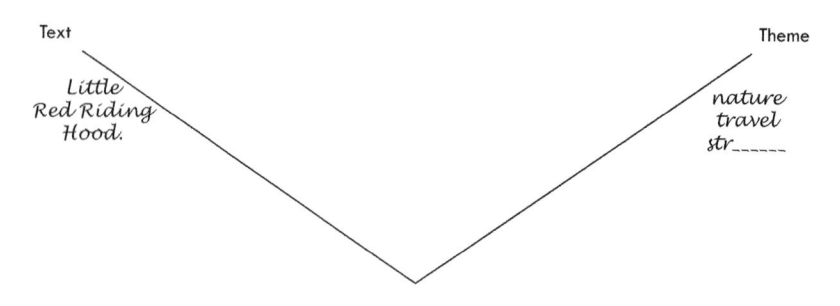

Little   *nature*
Red Riding   *travel*
Hood.   *str_____*

Figure 1.4

TIP

If students aren't sure if they have a theme, remind them that a theme is a noun. They can check this by testing a word in the 'talk show host' sentence starter:

On today's show we're going to be talking about _____.

Give this tip to struggling students, so they can check that they have potential themes listed.

Now it's time to narrow down our themes.

Ask students which two themes they think are the weakest and place a line through them (maybe themes like fashion, travel might go first). Go through the list again and ask, which two themes are stronger? Circle these (family, nature or strangers might stand out as more important or relevant). Continue this, alternating between striking off two weak themes and keeping two strong themes, until you have two to five themes left.

By the time students have finished prioritising the strengths of the themes, the schema might look a little like figure 1.5. Don't worry if the original list is much longer, so long as it is culled to a handful of themes.

These discussions also provide an opportunity to address some vocabulary. You can define the themes for the class and check understanding. You might want some students to write them down too.

These lists could also be used as a source for students struggling with decoding and spelling. Students who have higher literacy needs might benefit from copying the entire list (weak and strong themes). This list could then be used to support their reading comprehension and decoding. In small groups, these lists can be used as a source for vocabulary practice. Teachers and other professionals can apply phonological awareness and decoding activities to word lists.

For an extension or homework task, students might choose five more texts, perhaps more fairy tales, and practise writing the schema in their workbooks for each text, labelling the text on the left and listing the themes on the right.

A Way to Analyse Texts 25

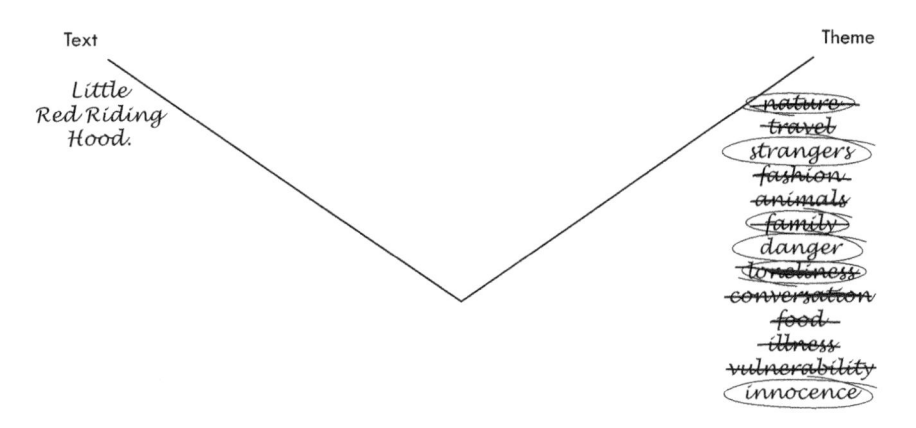

```
Text                                            Theme
Little                                         ~~nature~~
Red Riding                                     ~~travel~~
Hood.                                          (strangers)
      \                           /            ~~fashion~~
       \                         /             ~~animals~~
        \                       /              ~~family~~
         \                     /               (danger)
          \                   /                ~~loneliness~~
           \                 /                 ~~conversation~~
            \               /                  ~~food~~
             \             /                   ~~illness~~
              \           /                    ~~vulnerability~~
               \         /                     (innocence)
                \       /
                 \     /
                  \   /
                   \ /
                    V
```

Figure 1.5

Analysing Themes in Texts

Analysing with the Basic Text + Theme Schema

Let's consider our version of *Little Red Riding Hood* again and revisit our prioritised list in figure 1.6.

In 1.6 we're left with the themes *strangers*, *danger* and *innocence*.

Now students can start to craft some evaluative statements, by asking the question: What is the text saying about the theme(s)?

This is a straightforward question. At times it is easy to answer, and other times the answer is not so obvious, but at least we have a basic strategy to approach texts in an analytical way, and we can apply this question to any text.

Answers to the question could look like what we have in figure 1.7.

Some students might like to combine a couple of these statements to make a single comment like the one in figure 1.8.

Next, we'll examine another story like *Little Red Riding Hood*.

Students might like to know that texts can share themes, but the texts can reveal very different things about them. It's the information we gather and what we infer from the text that allows us to interpret themes differently. In this case, the information we interpret is about the characters, what they do and what happens consequently—the plot.

Students can now consider this story.

> *Little Blue Riding Boots*
>
> Once upon a time, in a little shack on the edge of a dark forest lived a little girl. One day she decided to visit her ailing grandmother. Grandma lived far away, and the only path was through the dark woods. The girl's father packed some food. Her mother gave her a pair of blue boots for the rough journey, then the little girl set off through the forest.

26 A Way to Analyse Texts

Text → Little Red Riding Hood.

What is the text saying about the theme(s)?

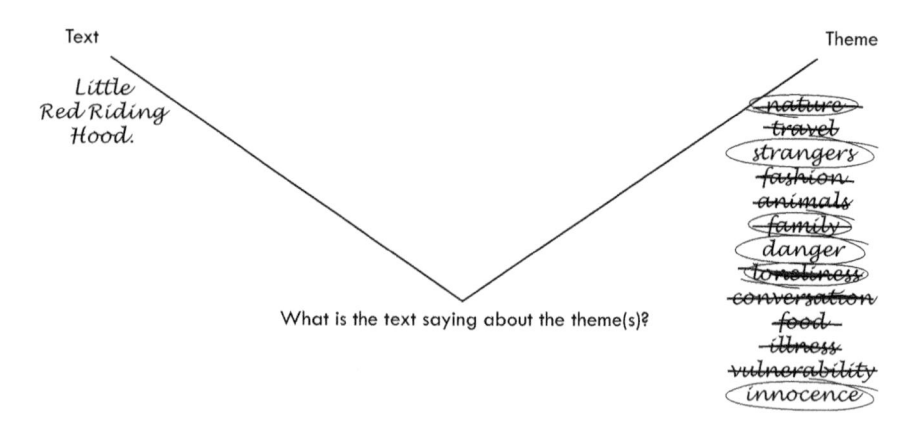

Theme:
- ~~nature~~
- ~~travel~~
- strangers
- ~~fashion~~
- ~~animals~~
- ~~family~~
- danger
- ~~loneliness~~
- ~~conversation~~
- ~~food~~
- ~~illness~~
- vulnerability
- innocence

Figure 1.6

Text → Little Red Riding Hood.

What is the text saying about the theme(s)?

The *innocent* can be easily influenced.
Travelling alone can be fraught with *danger*.
Don't talk to *strangers* because bad things can happen.

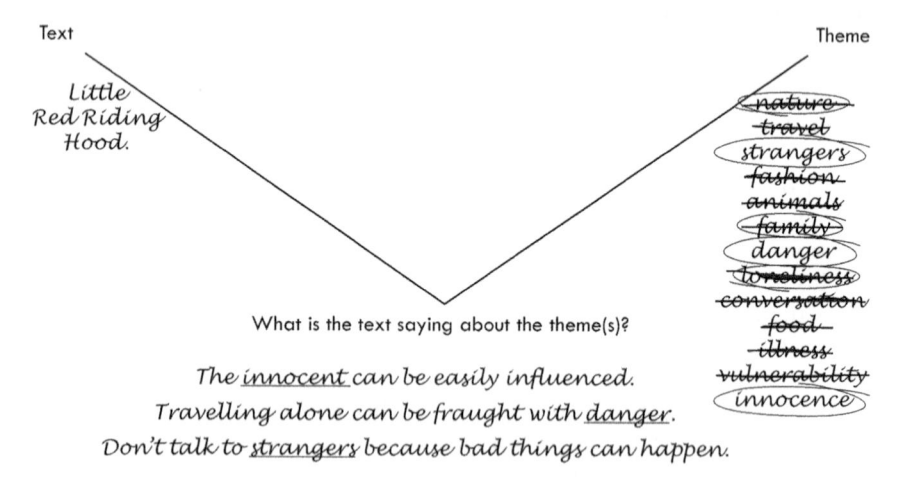

Theme:
- ~~nature~~
- ~~travel~~
- strangers
- ~~fashion~~
- ~~animals~~
- ~~family~~
- danger
- ~~loneliness~~
- ~~conversation~~
- ~~food~~
- ~~illness~~
- vulnerability
- innocence

Figure 1.7

The world can be fraught with danger for the innocent willing to put their trust in strangers.

Figure 1.8

After a time, the girl stopped to rest. As she sat, the bushes rustled. A wolf appeared, raised on his back legs. Startled, the little girl jumped, dropping her basket.

"Don't be afraid," said the wolf. "I won't harm you." The wolf looked at the basket. "What's in there?"

"None of your business," she replied, snatching up her basket.

The wolf frowned, "No need to be rude. I was just curious. These woods are lonely. I only meant to acquaint myself with you in the hope of some polite conversation, but never mind." The wolf turned to leave.

"Wait," said the little girl. "I do not mean to be impolite." The wolf turned and smiled. She continued, "I have food in the basket, for my grandma. She is old and ill and I am on my way to her now."

"Oh," said the wolf, "I'm sorry to hear your grandma is ill. Have you travelled far to see her?"

"Yes, but I still have a way to go, yet!"

"How far exactly?"

The little girl explained to the wolf exactly how far, and where, she had to go. The wolf shook his head. "That does sound like a long way. You'd best be off then. Thank you for the conversation." And with that, the little girl waved the wolf goodbye and continued her journey. "What a nice wolf," she thought.

When the little girl arrived at grandma's house, the door was already open. Fearing the worst, she rushed inside and to her relief, found grandma sitting at the table sipping hot chocolate, and there, opposite her, sat the wolf with a mug in his hand.

"Come in darling! I have some great news," said grandma. "This lovely wolf is a rich philanthropist. When you told him I was unwell, he came to visit. When I told him about my expensive medical bills, he offered to pay them."

The wolf smiled at the little girl, "You must care very much about your grandma to travel so far, all alone, and for that I would also like to move your grandma closer to you, so you can all be together."

The little girl didn't know what to say, she was so overcome with joy. She ran and embraced her grandmother. The wolf smiled. They drank tea and ate biscuits. And they all lived happily ever after.

As you can see, this is a silly distortion of *Little Red Riding Hood*. It has similar themes: nature, travel, family, strangers and so on. Perhaps the only theme missing is danger.

When students apply these themes to the scaffold, it will look similar to our last text, but what will change is the answers to the question at the base of the basic schema. Try working with your students to generate some points based on the themes. See figure 1.9 for an example.

Some students might feel confident enough to pair their comments like the example in figure 1.10. This is an opportunity for further editing. Students can look for synonyms, shorten some sentences into phrases, and combine them using conjunctions.

Choose some poems and short stories and see if students can apply the scaffold to the texts. There are some very short stories (micro fiction) and poems at the end of Chapter 2 that you could use. There are some one-page short stories in the Appendix also specifically for students to practise applying the schema.

Text | Theme

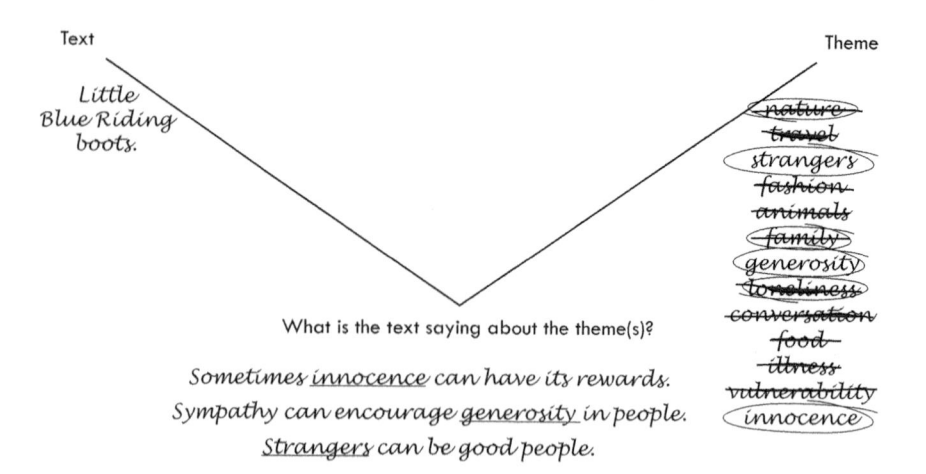

Little Blue Riding boots.

What is the text saying about the theme(s)?

Sometimes innocence can have its rewards.
Sympathy can encourage generosity in people.
Strangers can be good people.

~~nature~~
~~travel~~
strangers
~~fashion~~
~~animals~~
~~family~~
generosity
~~loneliness~~
~~conversation~~
~~food~~
~~illness~~
~~vulnerability~~
innocence

Figure 1.9

Trusting strangers is risky but can have its rewards.

Figure 1.10

Don't forget to let students know that movies, paintings, comic books and TV shows are also texts, and students can use these to practise. Short films are convenient and fun texts to deconstruct in a lesson. Pixar shorts are great for this and are usually accessible online or can be purchased through app stores.

Students with significantly lower language skills or other disabilities might want to start with animated shorts or picture books. Students struggling with literacy, who are otherwise typically developing, can apply this strategy to more sophisticated picture books—anything by Sean Tan is appropriate for this purpose.

TIP

For students with limited verbal expression, you can try recasting what they've said, then encourage them to write what you have modelled.

For students who are struggling to express themselves at all, who are silent, you can offer slightly different, and simple, binary choices. Your student can then choose an answer from the two you've offered, and you can move forward. The student will also have a response they can own and shape.

See the Appendix for Some Oral Language Supports.

Some students might feel comfortable to continue using this schema, and you might eventually withdraw it altogether for other students, but there might be students who require more detailed scaffolding, or more specific accommodations. So, if some students are still struggling, don't worry; the schema is about to become more scaffolded and targeted.

Using the Text + Theme schema is also an opportunity to gather some data: teachers might ask, which students succeeded with the schema application, and who is still struggling? What are they struggling with? Where are they getting stuck? Which students could say the answer, but struggled to get it down on paper? Which students couldn't do it at all? Answers to these types of questions can assist you to identify common difficulties and form small groups for targeted support, or identify students to refer for specialist evaluation or support. Student performance can also assist with writing goals for individual education plans and identify areas requiring more intensive supports, which we will cover.

Next we'll look at some additional scaffolding for this task.

Scaffolded Text + Theme Schema

You might like to start by defining 'neutral' to make sure students understand the term, then move on to the application of the next scaffold in figure 1.11.

To demonstrate this extended schema (figure 1.11), we will use *Romeo and Juliet* as our text and use 'love' as our theme. Our answers to the additional questions in this extended schema might look something like the ones in figure 1.12. Figure 1.13 offers an example of what the text could be saying about the theme.

The additional questions help students to get something down on paper. And this basic level of analysis is fine for students just starting out with essay writing, or students with language and learning difficulties who struggle to do anything else with a text but retell some of the plot or name some characters. At least this way they can start to make evaluative comments, even if they are very basic.

Text — Theme

1. Do you think the text is saying something good, bad or neutral about the theme?

2. Why? What happens in the text to make you think this?

What is the text saying about the theme(s)?

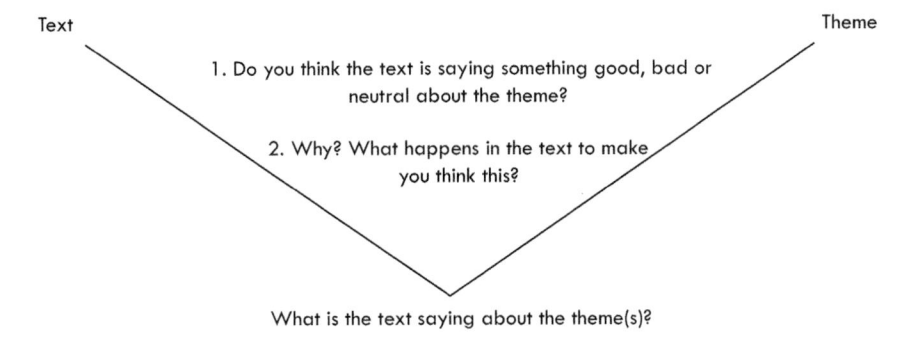

Figure 1.11

1. *Both, but I might focus on the bad aspects in the play for the moment.*

2. *The two main characters, Romeo and Juliet, fall in love but they ignore that their families are fighting and that Juliet has a fiance, and they lie to their parents.*

Figure 1.12

The text shows that love is so powerful it can override everything else.

Figure 1.13

If you find some students struggling with the second question, then they might need some additional support with basic text recall and will benefit from further scaffolding. You could provide the following cause-and-effect schema to support students who need to work through and document what happens in the text.

For a narrative text, a cause-and-effect scaffold could follow this sequence:

Do you think the text might be saying something good, bad or neutral about the theme?
Which event are you thinking of?
Which characters are involved?
What do they want?
What do they do?
What is the consequence of their actions?
Why is this good, bad or neutral?

Once students have answered some or all these questions, they can refer to their answers as they continue to work through the extended Text + Theme schema. Some students might need to map their recall onto a cause-and-effect schema each time they need to apply the extended scaffold to explore a theme in a text or book chapter. I have included a template in the Appendix (called Cause and Effect Scaffold) containing the questions above and some suggested sentence starters.

Defining Strategy

It is good practice to define our themes as we go, but we might consider some themes so obvious that we don't bother. But when you've landed on a particular theme and wish students to write about it, you might start to consider that some well-known and overused words might have quite broad meanings. Struggling students can benefit from definitions of even the most common words and phrases.

If we take *Romeo and Juliet* as our example, and our theme is 'love,' we can start by defining love. The number of entries I found in the dictionary was vast, so I chose the most relevant entries so I could focus on a particular aspect of love.

Love

> "a feeling of strong or constant affection for a person."
> "a person you love in a romantic way."
>
> (Merriam-Webster.com, 2021)

The Merriam-Webster online dictionary seems to define most words using relatively simple language, and because it is online students can click for more examples of their word in sentences. Collins Cobuild dictionaries also provide simple explanations. You might also decide to work with students to shape definitions they can all understand and agree on.

Now we have our definition, we have something to consider other than our initial understanding. It also means we can say more about the theme. If we choose "a person you love . . ." to answer our extended scaffold questions, then perhaps now, students can do something like the example in figure 1.14 for the extended questions 1 and 2.

So, what is the text saying about the theme?

1. Definitely something good and bad.

2. Well, the two main characters, Romeo and Juliet, fall in love and this makes them happy, like they are the only two people in the universe. They act as if they are each other's whole world, but this means that they ignore everything else around them in their single focus on each other. Also, because the people around them, their family and friends, do not approve of their romance, then they are forced to keep it secret, which ultimately results in their death.

Figure 1.14

One thing the text might be saying is that the success of Romeo and Juliet's romantic relationship depends largely on more than just their feelings. It needs to be acceptable to society and those closest to them to succeed.

So maybe, the text shows romantic love is doomed to fail if others don't approve.

Figure 1.15

Defining the theme allows students to hone their thoughts and be a little more specific. This can be pre-taught, but it can also become a permanent step in the task, so it becomes routine for students to define their terms.

Now it's time for students to try. Choose a text (it can be a poem, short story, or picture book). See if students can define the theme you set. Students could populate a graphic organiser, like a mind map or table, with reasons why they think the text is saying something good or bad about the theme. There are some examples in figure 1.16.

Students could also use this brainstorming activity as a reference while they work through the extended scaffold.

TIP

Students can also use idioms and proverbs to explore what the text is saying about the theme.

You might find 1–3 sayings pertaining to a theme. Explain their meanings, then students can discuss how this might apply (or not) to the text.

Try searching the internet for quotes on themes.

Try using e-book versions of proverb and idiom dictionaries to word search.

Pairs Strategy

This time we'll pair themes, then decide what the text is saying about each pair. It supports a more detailed analysis by considering how certain ideas relate to each other.

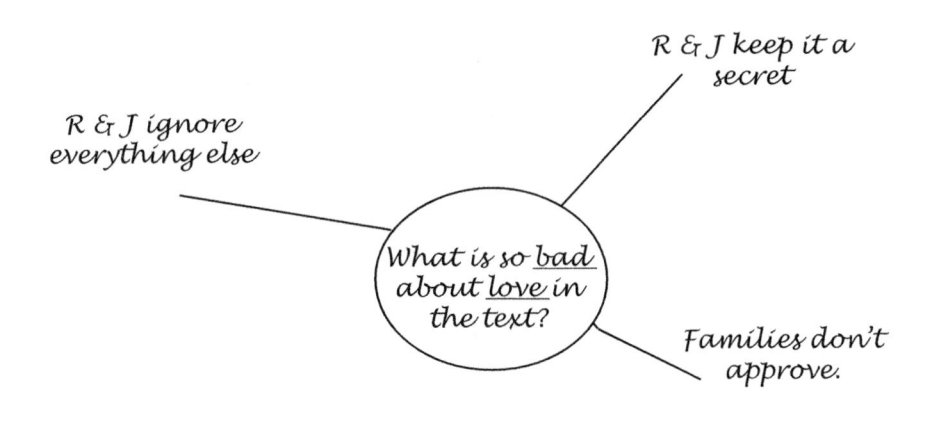

```
                                    R & J keep it a
                                      secret
                                     /
   R & J ignore
   everything else
                  \
                   ( What is so bad )
                   ( about love in  )
                   (   the text?    )
                                    \
                                     Families don't
                                       approve.
```

What's so bad about love in the text?	What's so good about love in the text?
R & J ignore everything else	They are dedicated to each other
They keep it a secret	
Their families don't approve	

Figure 1.16

We will use *The Giver* by Lois Lowry (2008) for this example. See figure 1.17.

If students aren't sure how to start some of these comments, there's a list of suggestions for sentence starters in figure 1.18. It might help to stick them up on the wall, or have students who need them, write some in the back of their notebooks for future reference. Some of the sentence starters might also spark students' thoughts on a theme or topic and get them writing. And I've left some room for you and your students to add to the list.

A Way to Analyse Texts

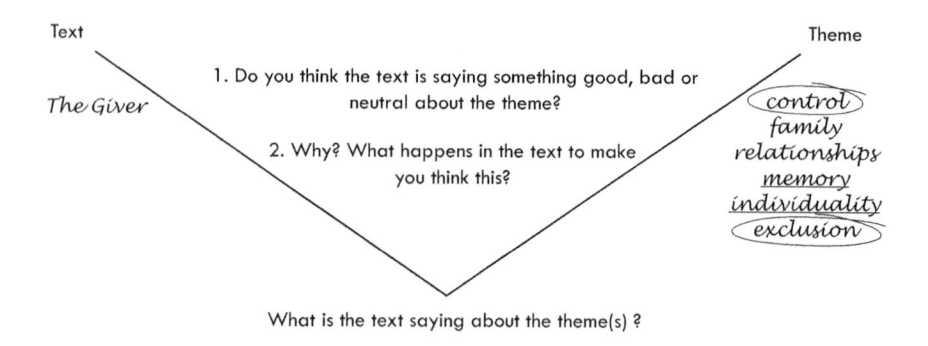

Text — The Giver

1. Do you think the text is saying something good, bad or neutral about the theme?

2. Why? What happens in the text to make you think this?

Theme — (control), family, relationships, memory, individuality, (exclusion)

What is the text saying about the theme(s) ?

control & Exclusion
If societies control and exclude people who are different, that can cause harm to those excluded and can repress variety by favouring sameness.

memory & individuality
Taking away peoples's memories might protect them from bad things but this can also take away their individuality and identity.

control & relationships
By controlling who lives together, the society also control feelings and this means no one can form close and meaningful relationships.

Figure 1.17

TIP

If the question 'What is the text saying about the theme?' is too hard, try:
  'What do the actions of the characters *teach* you about __(theme)__?'
Students who are still struggling with this question might try:
  'If there was a moral to the story about __(theme)__, what do you think it could be?'

Syntactic Scaffold

Now that we have our scaffolded schemas, and a variety of ways to approach answering them, students might find that working through them makes

Even though...
If...
Sometimes...
Just because...
No matter what...
By...
People can...

_____
_____
_____
_____
_____

Figure 1.18

identifying themes and evaluating the text easier. Although you might still find some students know what they want to say, but still can't get it down on paper.

Now might be the time to give those students a quick grammar lesson. Let's go back to nouns for a minute.

NOUN

A person, place or thing.

Remind students that *every* item and person they see is a noun, and a whole heap of things they don't see can be nouns too, abstract things like ideas, concepts, topics . . . and themes.

Do you remember this tip?

> **TIP**
>
> If you aren't sure if you have a theme, remember a theme is a noun. You can check this by testing your word in the 'talk show host' sentence starter:
>
> On today's show we're going to be talking about _____.

36   *A Way to Analyse Texts*

If your theme fits here, then list it; if not, see if you can change it so it sounds like it does.

This is our noun test. You will hear students say, hang on! I can end that sentence with words like 'running' and 'building' and they're verbs, doing words, right? And yes, we know those words can also be verbs, but students need to know if they are talking about them as a topic, then the verbs become a 'thing,' and therefore, a noun.

If they're still struggling, then demonstrate the following for them. If they can complete the following sentence placing a word before 'is/are' then a quality (adjective) after 'is/are,' then they have a noun:

(the)_____ is/are _____.

Once students get the hang of this, they can explore verbs. You might start by providing a definition for them. Here's mine: A verb tells you what the noun is doing, being or having.

You could get students active to demonstrate the definition. You could ask them to stand, then instruct students do these things as you read each word.

wave
laugh
clap
tap

When demonstrating verbs, I like to make two columns on the board or on a notepad, label the first one 'doing verbs', then ask students for more examples. As you can imagine the list gets large very quickly. I explain we must stop because there are so many doing verbs that we could fill the board and then start on the walls, and we'd be there writing examples for years. The other column, for being verbs, ends up much shorter.

The next group of words are those which show what the noun is being. You could try the activity again, asking students to do the actions as you say them.

laugh
clap
tap
is

Maybe tell them that even though they couldn't do 'is,' it doesn't mean that it is not a verb. Students should know there are verbs that, on their own, have little to do with actions. They are a very small group. There's some examples in figure 1.19. See the Appendix for more.

A Way to Analyse Texts 37

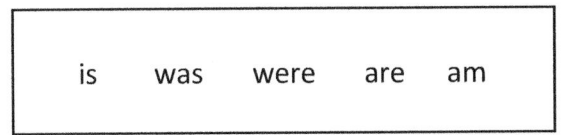

is   was   were   are   am

Figure 1.19

We can teach students to classify these verbs as *being* verbs because, on their own, they simply state what something, somewhere or someone is 'being,' or simply when or where they are.

The forest <u>is</u> dark.
The woman <u>was</u> overjoyed.
I <u>am</u> hungry.

If you want to provide students more practice with this, you could try the following:

1. Have students find an item, from their desk, in the room.
2. Demonstrate by holding out your item. For example, a book: *This book is small*, then flick through the pages and say, *I can <u>turn</u> the pages*.
3. In pairs, students could say two things about their item: What the item is <u>being</u>, and what you <u>do</u> with it.
4. Ask students to write down their sentences and underline which <u>being</u> verb they used, and which <u>doing</u> verb they used.

You could revisit this task the next day. Students could refer to their sentences and tell you, one at a time, what they *did* yesterday, changing the tense of their verb. You might also discuss why they can't necessarily say the same thing about their other sentence: The pencil case will still *be* red today; whereas yesterday, they might have said, 'The pencil *is* on the desk,' today they might say 'yesterday, it *was* on the desk.'

We could go on about nouns and verbs some more, but this is all students need to understand for now.

Students are going to use this information about nouns and verbs to respond to our next Text + Theme schema. They can respond by starting with one of the smallest sentences we can work with: a noun, and a verb.

As students might have gathered from examining our being verbs, they need to be followed by something. 'The chairs are' is not a sentence. The sentence must be finished by 'red', or maybe 'broken,' something that describes what state the chairs are in.

Students might like to know that doing verbs animate the noun, make it do something, like a hand operating a puppet. This can include having the noun doing something to something else.

The dog hit the cat.

Or maybe, doing something somewhere.

The dog ran in the park.

Or just doing something.

The dog ran.

This last example is simply 'noun + verb'—This is an example of an intransitive verb that doesn't take an object. These are the sentence structures students can start with.

Students can use the column scaffold in figure 1.20 for constructing simple sentences. They can animate the nouns sitting in the left column, by placing a doing verb on the right. Once students have done this, then they can try to elaborate to the right of their sentence. I've already elaborated on a couple (in grey).

noun	verb
Leaves	*rustle in the wind.*
The water	*trickled*
Love	*endures*
Faith	*comforts people.*
Dogs	
The classroom	
Many hands	
Money	
Belonging	
Loneliness	

Figure 1.20

You might like to remind your students themes are also nouns and, in the same way students have elaborated on the nouns in the noun|verb scaffold, they can also pair themes with verbs.

I'll demonstrate how this might look if we used *Burial Rites* by Hannah Kent (2014) in figure 1.21. The themes are not exhaustive, so feel free to add any if you are familiar with the novel. There is a summary of this text in the Appendix for those who aren't. We will use our themes as our nouns and then animate them with a verb.

Note in figure 1.21 how I've avoided 'is' and other being verbs in favour of doing verbs. This is not always necessary, but it does assist with building students' vocabularies with interesting verbs. It also makes the task concrete and visual; students can personify the themes and 'see' them in action.

Students can use negatives like 'doesn't,' 'don't,' and 'won't' before their verbs. Students can also use words like 'sometimes' and 'can' before the verb if they wish. I have underlined the main verbs in figure 1.22 so you can see them and the types of words surrounding them.

Using 'can' to kick-start the verb phrase might also help students move things along.

Students might not be entirely happy with all their sentences. Some sentences might be too general, while others might not really say what students

Text — Theme

Burial Rites

1. Do you think the text is saying something good, bad or neutral about the theme?

2. Why? What happens in the text to make you think this?

belonging
justice
punishment
prejudice
class differences
family
loss

What is the text saying about the theme(s)?

noun	verb
Belonging	**can provide** fulfilment.
Justice	**abandons** those who don't have a voice.
Punishment	**doesn't always fit** the crime.
Prejudice	**influences** behaviour.
Class difference	**can foster** discrimination.
Family	**exists** beyond the bonds of blood.

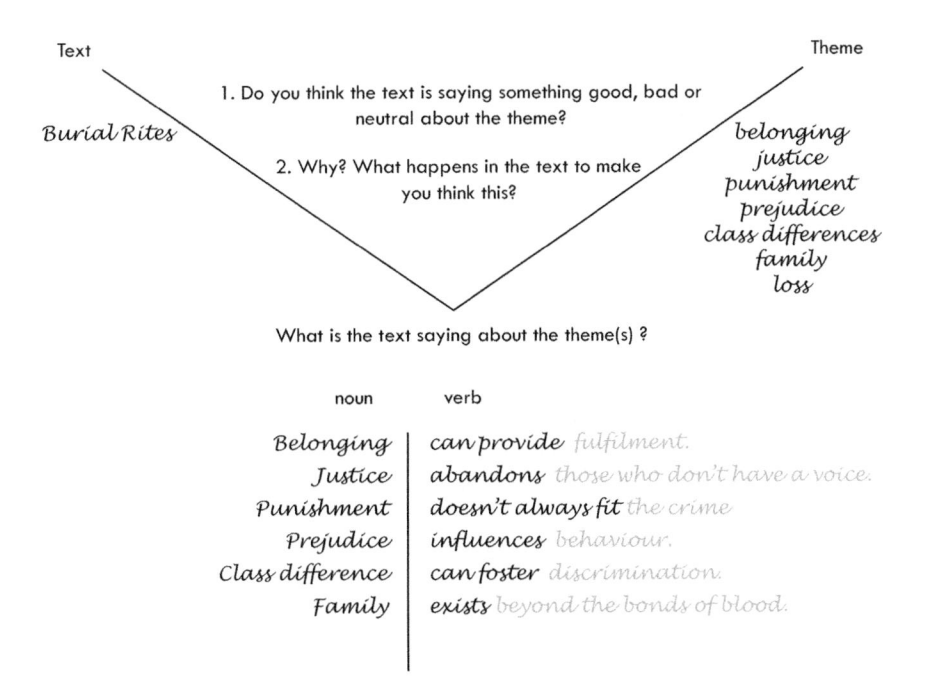

Figure 1.21

noun	verb
Belonging	can *provide* fulfilment.
Justice	*abandons* those who don't have a voice.
Punishment	doesn't always *fit* the crime.
Prejudice	*influences* behaviour.
Class difference	can *foster* discrimination.
Family	*exists* beyond the bonds of blood.

Figure 1.22

noun	verb
~~Belonging~~	~~can provide fulfilment.~~
Justice	*abandons* those who don't have a voice.
The Punishment	doesn't always *fit* the crime.
Prejudice	*influences* behaviour.
Class difference	can *foster* discrimination.
Family	*exists* beyond the bonds of blood.
People	*belong* where they find acceptance

Figure 1.23

want. If this is the case, then they can take the sentences they don't like and change some of the nouns into verbs. Then they can rustle up some nouns to go with the verbs to say things about the text. They can ask 'What is doing the verb?' For example, 'What or who belongs?' See figure 1.23.

Students can use being verbs, *is* or the less certain *can be*, but try to limit this practice or students might start to rely on these verbs too often. It might help to tell students to use being verbs only after they have tried but failed to pair their theme with a doing verb.

I have only chosen a few nouns (themes) to do this in figure 1.24.

Students can also combine some of their being and doing verb sentences. If they need to, they can also add some words to their nouns (maybe *the*, *an*, *a*). To demonstrate, I have joined four of our sentences (using *and*) in figure 1.25.

A Way to Analyse Texts 41

noun	verb
Beonging	
Justice	<u>is</u> remote for women and the poor.
Punishment	<u>can be</u> disproportionate to the crime.
Prejudice	
Class difference	
Family	

Figure 1.24

Justice can abandon those who don't have a voice <u>and</u> is remote for women and the poor.

The punishment doesn't always fit the crime <u>and</u> is not always proportionate.

Figure 1.25

In the text, justice abandons those who don't have a voice and is remote for women and the marginalised, like Agnes.

Burial Rites shows the punishment doesn't always fit the crime and is not proportionate.

Figure 1.26

    Students can then polish their comments. The only other thing I would do to some of the sentences is add the following prepositional phrase: *In the text...*

    Following these adjustments, students could make some of the comments a little more specific to the text. I have made my changes and additions in grey in figure 1.26.

Cumulative Strategy

A cumulative strategy centers on one theme first, so students can say something basic about the text right away, then build on this by adding layers of complexity. I've demonstrated this process using *Maus* by Art Spiegelman (1997) in figure 1.27.

Using the scaffolded Text + Theme schema, students start with a theme and ask if the text is saying something good, bad or neutral about it, then write down their answer at the base of the schema.

Next, students ask, 'what has this got to do with the next theme?'

Students using this strategy will continue to ask this question, building their commentary, until they have something they are happy with.

Once you have identified the level of scaffolding that works for each student, and identified strategies that work for them, you might like to practice the Text + Theme schema using a prescribed text, maybe one chapter, or a poem, to begin with.

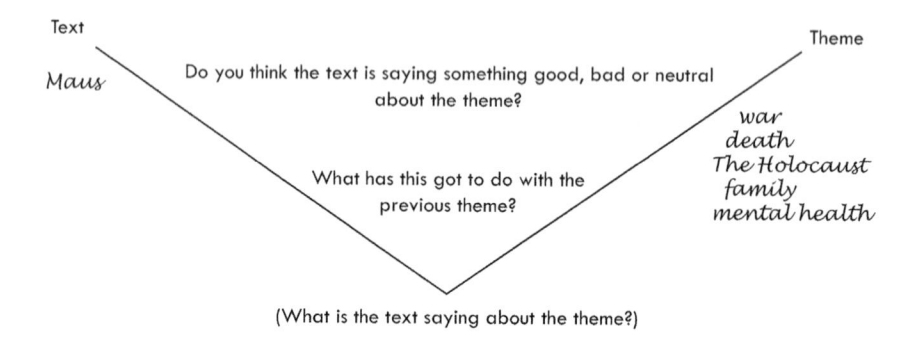

Text — *Maus*

Do you think the text is saying something good, bad or neutral about the theme?

Theme
- war
- death
- The Holocaust
- family
- mental health

What has this got to do with the previous theme?

(What is the text saying about the theme?)

War is bad.

What has this got to do with *death*?

War is bad because it causes unnecessary death.

What has this got to do with *The Holocaust*?

The Holocaust resulted in the senseless and untimely death of millions of Jewish people during WWII.

What has this got to do with *loss*?

The Holocaust resulted in the death of millions and the loss of family members.

What has this got to do with *mental Health*?

In addition to the senseless death of millions and the untimely loss of loved ones, the Holocaust was responsible for significant mental health issues among survivors.

Figure 1.27

In the next chapter we're going to look at essay scaffolds, not just for the whole essay, but for the parts. And I know, you have seen a ton of essay scaffolds, but these are a bit different.

We will continue applying the skills students have learnt in this chapter while they learn to build paragraphs, starting with asking 'what is the text saying about the theme?' From here, we will build the essay using what we will call steering questions, which are designed to gently steer students through writing an essay-style paragraph for any given text.

References

Alvermann, D. E. (1981). The compensatory effect of graphic organizers on descriptive text. *The Journal of Educational Research (Washington, D.C.)*, *75*(1), 44–48. https://doi.org/10.1080/00220671.1981.10885354

Dexter, D. D., & Hughes, C. A. (2011). Graphic organizers and students with learning disabilities: A meta-analysis. *Learning Disability Quarterly*, *34*(1), 51–72. https://doi.org/10.1177/073194871103400104

Kent, H. (2014). *Burial rites* (Picador edition 2014. ed.). Picador.

Lowry, L. (2008). *The giver*. Harper Collins.

Merriam-Webster.com. (2021). Retrieved October 18, 2021, from https://www.merriam-webster.com

Spiegelman, A. (1997). *Maus: A survivor's tale* (1st ed.). Pantheon Books.

Swanson, H. L. (1999). Instructional components that predict treatment outcomes for students with learning disabilities: Support for a combined strategy and direct instruction model. *Learning Disabilities Research and Practice*, *14*(3), 129–140. https://doi.org/10.1207/sldrp1403_1

2 Essential Essay Structures

> Did You Know...
> There are greater demands on students to produce written texts that do not simply present knowledge but display opinion that is formed by knowledge and to show how they have arrived at their conclusions (Kellogg, 2008). Because expression at the secondary level is more demanding, then tasks that aim to improve this type of expression should be focused on curriculum tasks (Ehren, 2002).

English Essay Structure

Older students are learning that there are many structures that contribute to the successful composition of a piece of writing—the words chosen, the sentence structures, the organization of paragraphs. In this chapter we will focus on these elements as we dismantle the composition of an academic English essay. Figure 2.1 is a common schema for an essay text-type.

This is the basic structure, no detail. Each box represents a paragraph, and each box is labelled so students know what each paragraph is meant to achieve. No doubt teachers and tutors have seen a few of these, and speech pathologists working with secondary and tertiary students may have seen some too. It's straightforward and sequential, but the problem is it's not terribly helpful for showing students *how* to write an essay, and *how* to fill the boxes.

Some will look at a schema, like this one, and take it to mean that essays must be written in this sequence, starting with the introduction and then working through the rest, because this is how we read an essay. However, this doesn't mean it's the best way to write one. So, we will start with a detailed analysis of one of the major components. Instead of starting with the introduction, we'll start with the body paragraph and its structure.

There are a few good reasons I can think of to start with the body paragraph. First, it's difficult to write an introduction to something that hasn't been written. You can do it, but you'll have to go back and do some heavy editing later. While this might be okay for writing a thesis, or a textbook, the issue with

DOI: 10.4324/9781003263401-3

ENGLISH ESSAY STRUCTURE

Introduction
State your overall argument, and how you will break down that argument in your essay body paragraphs.

Essay Body Paragraph
Discuss one element of your argument, and provide examples and explanation to support it.

Essay Body Paragraph
Discuss one element of your argument, and provide examples and explanation to support it.

Essay Body Paragraph
Discuss one element of your argument, and provide examples and explanation to support it.

Conclusion
Restate your argument, and explain how your points have demonstrated it.

Figure 2.1

English essays for academic purposes is that sometimes they are written under timed conditions, on paper, with pen. In exams, it's tricky to go back and edit introductions. Crossing things out, adding stuff in the margins—this can get messy and chew up valuable minutes. Second, most of what you need to write short answers for English can be learnt by practising body paragraphs, so they have many uses. Third, they take longer to learn and master than introduction or conclusion paragraphs, so let's get them over with now.

The Body Paragraph

Let's have another look at the body paragraph and what's in it, starting with figure 2.2.

> **Essay Body Paragraph**
> Discuss one element of your argument, and provide examples and explanation to support it.

Figure 2.2

Part 1
Write a point, a sentence that supports your main argument.
Part 2
Explain your assertion in more detail or offer a rationale, a reason for making it.
Part 3
Provide an example or some evidence (a quote perhaps) that supports your point.
Part 4
Establish which techniques are used in the text: perhaps use your example to identify a language technique, or maybe two.
Part 5
Scrutinise the language and describe the effect of the technique.
Part 6
Link this information back to the original essay topic and the overall argument.

Figure 2.3

There's not a lot there to get students started. Most students will require more explanation than what we have in figure 2.2, so we will break down the components further. Figure 2.3 sets out one way you can structure the information in a body paragraph for all students.

The detailed paragraph structure might be enough for most students to work with, but you will probably find that students with language and learning difficulties will need further scaffolding to get something down on paper. In the

Part 1 What is the text saying about the theme?
Part 2 What happens in the text to make you think this?
Part 3 What is the best example (quote)?
Part 4 Is there a technique you can extract from the quote or elsewhere?
Part 5 What might the technique make the viewer *think* or *feel*?
Part 6 How does all of this support your argument?

Figure 2.4

first chapter, we scaffolded our understanding and analysis of themes in texts by asking questions. And we will do something similar here too.

Figure 2.4 follows the same structure as the previous two figures, but I've added some questions that address each segment of the body paragraph. The idea is that by answering these questions, students can write their entire paragraph. You might also notice that completing each component relies on the previous answer. This supports students to build cohesive texts.

We'll look at this in action in a little while, but for now, we need to make this structure easier to remember. To do this, I'll offer the following acronym, a mnemonic device to help us remember the structure and purpose of each component.

ACCESS Schema

We are using ACCESS here, but if you would like to adjust this acronym, feel free. PEEL and TEEL are common acronyms for the basic structure of a body paragraph for all subject areas.

There are variants on the aforementioned structures too, extended versions, specifically for English essay paragraphs which incorporate literary technique identification and analysis.

PETAL was one I came across in a Sydney school, where the T represented *technique*, and the A was for *analyse*. SEQAL was another, and stood for *state, explain, quote, analyse* and *link*. The one presented here is six letters because I have broken the paragraph into six components. Each component is named using a verb; the acronym tells students what to *do* in each section.

Each letter in ACCESS represents a function for each portion of the paragraph, provides direction for what needs to be done and supplies a question: students must *argue* their point of view, then *clarify* this view through explanation, then *confirm* all of this by providing evidence and quoting, then *extract* a literary technique from the example to support their argument, *scrutinise* the technique to explain its effect, then *synthesise* the information in the paragraph to draw a final conclusion that can be linked back to the main argument.

It will be helpful for students to know what the terms mean if they are to understand the function of each section of their paragraph. It's also another opportunity to expand their vocabulary. Students might want to write definitions for the ACCESS words in figure 2.5. You might also wish to help students to link the definitions with the sections in the scaffold the way I have done in figure 2.6.

The idea is that students can analyse and write about a text by using the Text + Theme schema, and any of the additional scaffolding from Chapter 1 to help answer the first question. Students can then go on to answer the subsequent questions.

ARGUE

CLARIFY

CONFIRM

EXTRACT

SCRUTINISE

SYNTHESISE

Figure 2.5

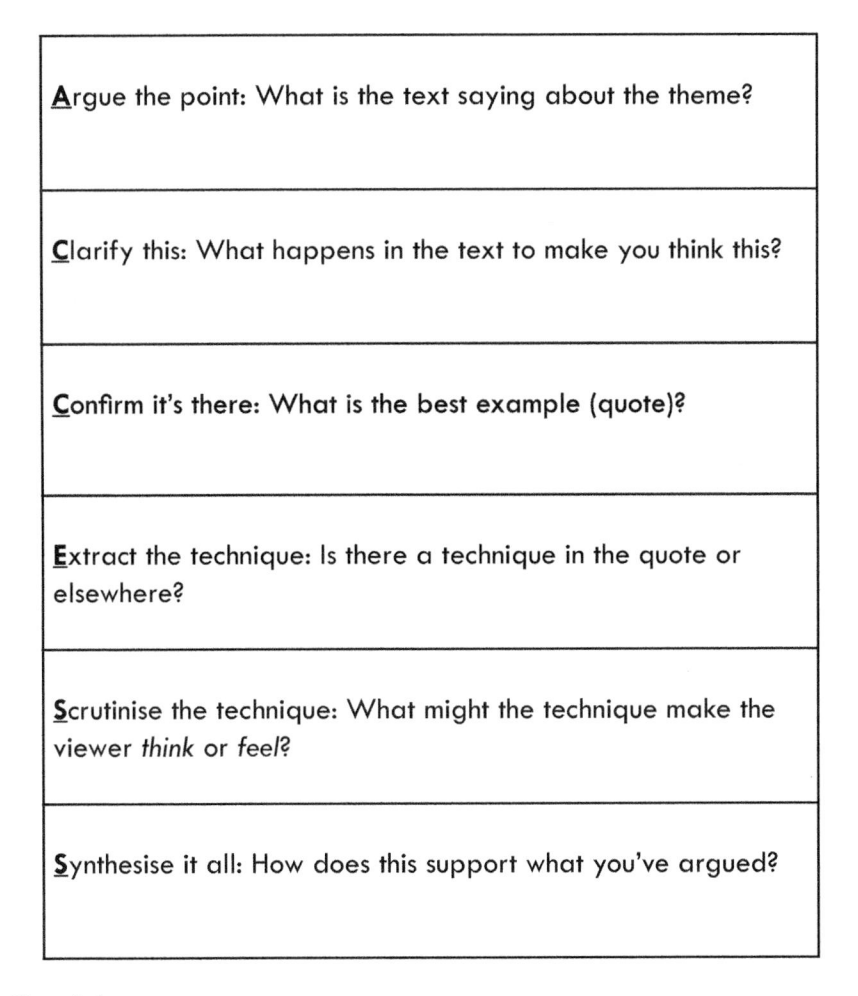

Argue the point: What is the text saying about the theme?
Clarify this: What happens in the text to make you think this?
Confirm it's there: What is the best example (quote)?
Extract the technique: Is there a technique in the quote or elsewhere?
Scrutinise the technique: What might the technique make the viewer *think* or *feel*?
Synthesise it all: How does this support what you've argued?

Figure 2.6

The following is an application of the process using a poem. I have selected one theme to write about. Students don't always have to write about more than one, and sometimes there are several things that can be said on just one theme.

A Poison Tree
by William Blake

I was angry with my friend:
I told my wrath, my wrath did end.
I was angry with my foe:
I told it not, my wrath did grow.

And I watered it in fears,
Night and morning with my tears;
And I sunned it with smiles,
And with soft deceitful wiles.
And it grew both day and night,
Till it bore an apple bright.
And my foe beheld it shine.
And he knew that it was mine,
And into my garden stole
When the night had veiled the pole;
In the morning glad I see
My foe outstretched beneath the tree.

If you use this example, you might like to draw students' attention to words like 'wrath' and 'foe' then define these. Students can highlight other words they might not know and write definitions in their notebooks or in the margins of the poem.

Now we have some commentary on the text, we can write a paragraph. I've chosen to open my paragraph with the second point. Notice how I've kept the ACCESS questions on the page in figure 2.8. If students have used the scaffolded schema with extended questions, then they can use their answer to '2. Why? What happens in the text to make you think this?' to answer the 'clarify' question.

Students can also type the ACCESS questions in a Word document and delete the questions once they've answered them. Students are then left with a paragraph of writing that adheres to an English essay paragraph structure.

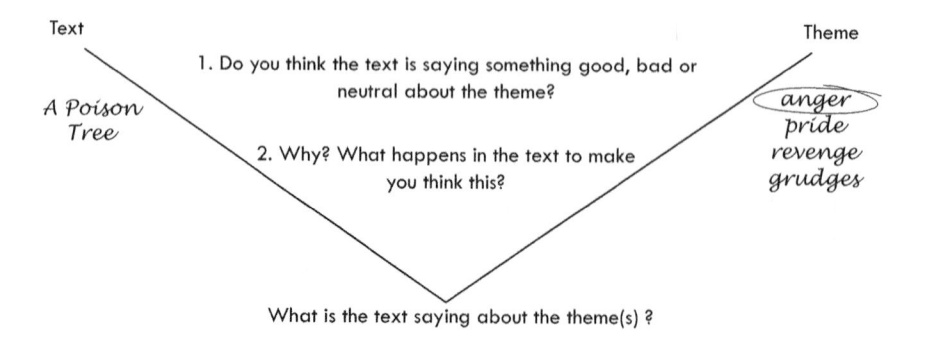

Text — Theme

A Poison Tree

1. Do you think the text is saying something good, bad or neutral about the theme?

2. Why? What happens in the text to make you think this?

What is the text saying about the theme(s)?

anger
pride
revenge
grudges

Anger is an emotion we all experience, but acknowledging it is healthy.

Anger can be destructive.

Figure 2.7

Argue: What is the text saying about the theme? *The text shows anger can be destructive.*
Clarify: What happens in the text to make you think this? *In the poem, the narrator is angry with a friend, but confronts it and feels better. When he gets angry with someone else, he dwells on it and ends up harming that person.*
Confirm: What is the best example (quote)? *The narrator describes what he did with his anger; "watered it in fears" and "sunned it with smiles."*
Extract technique: Is there a technique in the quote or elsewhere? *Here, the author uses metaphor and irony.*
Scrutinise: What might the technique make the viewer *think* or *feel*? *The verbs "watered" and "sunned" make the viewer think of anger being nurtured and growing like a plant. Imagery of plants growing is usually positive, but in the poem, this type of growth ends in harm, which is ironic.*
Synthesise: How does this support what you've argued? *Anger can grow and cause harm if you let it.*

Figure 2.8

By approaching texts this way, students are not only practising essay writing, but they're also studying and note taking. And depending on which goals you have set for students, you could also supply the additional scaffolds and strategies students require to build and understand narrative schema and vocabulary, and to formulate sentences.

You can find blank templates for the Text + Theme schema and the ACCESS essay body paragraph in the Appendix.

52 *Essential Essay Structures*

```
Theme                    Text

                                    ┌──────────────────────────────────────┐
                                    │ Argue: What is the text saying about the theme? │
                                    ├──────────────────────────────────────┤
What is the text saying about the theme(s)?  │ Clarify: What happens in the text to make you think this? │
                                    ├──────────────────────────────────────┤
                                    │ Confirm: What is the best example (quote)? │
                                    ├──────────────────────────────────────┤
                                    │ Extract technique: Is there a technique in the quote or elsewhere? │
                                    ├──────────────────────────────────────┤
                                    │ Scrutinise: What might the technique make the viewer *think* or *feel*? │
                                    ├──────────────────────────────────────┤
                                    │ Synthesise: How does this support what you've argued? │
                                    └──────────────────────────────────────┘
```

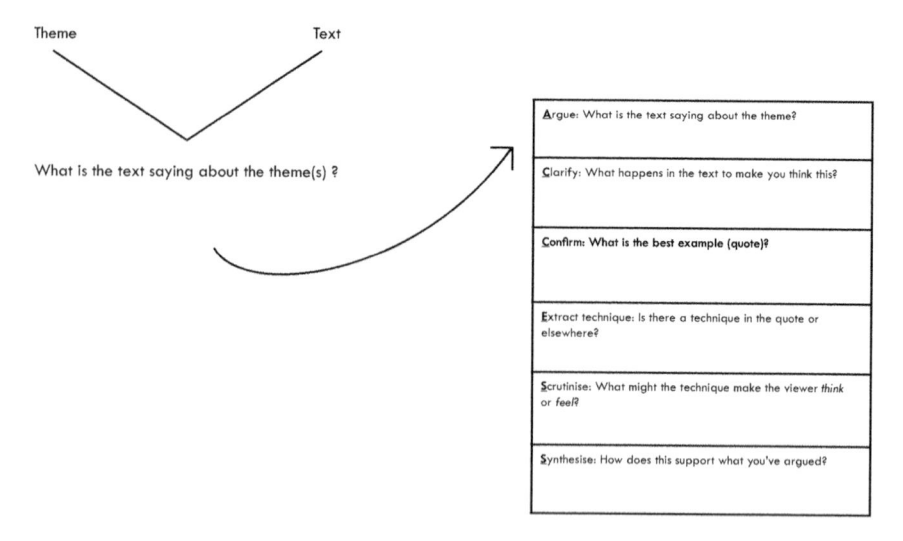

Figure 2.9

Texts and Excerpts for Practice

If you want to practice this process with students before you apply the scaffolds to a prescribed text, try applying them to some short stories, poems or picture books. You might like to show students a visual representation of how the two schemas that they have learned can be linked together (see figure 2.9).

Micro Fiction and Poems

Worksheets 2.1–2.11 are micro fictions (very short stories) and poems for students to practice the Text + Theme schema and the ACCESS paragraph scaffold. You can copy one of the Text + Theme schemas (in the Appendix) and add any additional strategies that work best for your students who are struggling.

Don't forget the cheat sheet in the Appendix, the sheet with definitions and examples of text-types, genres and themes. Some students might like to refer to the sheet to get ideas for potential themes.

If you aren't sure which texts to start with, the micro fiction texts are easier than the poetry texts, so keep this in mind when choosing one so it can be pitched at the right level. Feel free to choose your own short stories and poems, even for practise—the more relevant the content is to the curriculum, the better.

Worksheet

In the Dark

They snuck into the house and fumbled in the dark, whispering and shushing each other.

Someone turned a key in the door, then the hallway light was on. The intruders sunk further into their hiding spots. Did the man know they were there, lingering unseen in his house? The man hesitated a moment before venturing into the open darkness. He switched on the light.

The music started. Party poppers exploded. 'Surprise!' the intruders cried.

Argue: What is the text saying about the theme?

Clarify: What happens in the text to make you think this?

Confirm: What is the best example (quote)?

Extract technique: Is there a technique in the quote or elsewhere?

Scrutinise: What might the technique make the viewer *think* or *feel*?

Synthesise: How does this support what you've argued?

Worksheet 2.1

Worksheet

On Display

Sweat made her armpits itch, but she dared not scratch them, not now. She had her biggest audience yet.

The light was so hot, and so bright she could hardly make them out, but she knew they were there, silent, awaiting her performance.

She clicked to the first slide. 'Good morning class'.

'Good morning Ms. Cooper,' her audience mumbled in unison.

Argue: What is the text saying about the theme?

Clarify: What happens in the text to make you think this?

Confirm: What is the best example (quote)?

Extract technique: Is there a technique in the quote or elsewhere?

Scrutinise: What might the technique make the viewer *think* or *feel*?

Synthesise: How does this support what you've argued?

Worksheet 2.2

Worksheet

Pressure

'Scalpel!'

The nurse hands the surgeon his steel blade. His palms sweat, and hands shake. It could be fatigue. It's 9:01pm, his last procedure after a twenty-hour day.

The blade slips in his hand. A heartbeat slows then drops away to nothing. There's a flatline, but it doesn't show on the monitor.

The patient's surgery was successfully rescheduled. The surgeon was pronounced dead at 9:10pm. Heart failure.

Argue: What is the text saying about the theme?

Clarify: What happens in the text to make you think this?

Confirm: What is the best example (quote)?

Extract technique: Is there a technique in the quote or elsewhere?

Scrutinise: What might the technique make the viewer *think* or *feel*?

Synthesise: How does this support what you've argued?

Worksheet 2.3

Worksheet

Stalker

He'd been standing on the other side of the door for over an hour, but it felt more like days.

He'd been thinking about what he'd say when she opened the door, thinking should he knock again, call out to her, text her. He knows first impressions count.

What the heck, he thought. Just go for it.

He shoved the pantry door outwards and shot across the kitchen, covering her mouth before she could scream.

Argue: What is the text saying about the theme?

Clarify: What happens in the text to make you think this?

Confirm: What is the best example (quote)?

Extract technique: Is there a technique in the quote or elsewhere?

Scrutinise: What might the technique make the viewer *think* or *feel*?

Synthesise: How does this support what you've argued?

Worksheet 2.4

Worksheet

First Impressions

She sat around all day, then sat around all night. She rolled into bed, then rolled out each morning, only to sit around some more.

In fact, she's been sitting around most of her life.

And next year, she'll sit around some more, in Rio, where she'll ride her wheelchair to Paralympic glory.

Argue: What is the text saying about the theme?

Clarify: What happens in the text to make you think this?

Confirm: What is the best example (quote)?

Extract technique: Is there a technique in the quote or elsewhere?

Scrutinise: What might the technique make the viewer *think* or *feel*?

Synthesise: How does this support what you've argued?

Worksheet 2.5

Worksheet

A Singer of the Bush
Banjo Paterson

There is a waving of grass in the breeze
And a song in the air,
And the murmur of myriad bees
That toil everywhere.
There is scent in the blossom and bough,
And the breath of the spring
Is as soft as a kiss on the brow
And springtime I sing.

There is drought on the land, and the stock
Tumble down in their tracks
Or follow a tottering flock
The scrub-cutter's axe.
While ever a creature survives
The axes shall swing
We are fighting with fate for their lives
And the combat I sing.

Argue: What is the text saying about the theme?

Clarify: What happens in the text to make you think this?

Confirm: What is the best example (quote)?

Extract technique: Is there a technique in the quote or elsewhere?

Scrutinise: What might the technique make the viewer *think* or *feel*?

Synthesise: How does this support what you've argued?

Worksheet 2.6

Worksheet

Grief
Elizabeth Barrett Browning

I tell you; hopeless grief is passionless,
That only men incredulous of despair,
Half-taught in anguish, through the midnight air
Beat upward to God's throne in loud access
Of shrieking and reproach. Full desert-ness,
In souls as countries, lieth silent-bare
Under the blanching, vertical eye-glare
Of the absolute heavens. Deep-hearted man, express
Grief for thy dead in silence like to death
Most like a monumental statue set
In everlasting watch and moveless woe
Till itself crumble to the dust beneath.
Touch it; the marble eyelids are not wet:
If it could weep, it could rise and go.

Argue: What is the text saying about the theme?

Clarify: What happens in the text to make you think this?

Confirm: What is the best example (quote)?

Extract technique: Is there a technique in the quote or elsewhere?

Scrutinise: What might the technique make the viewer *think* or *feel*?

Synthesise: How does this support what you've argued?

Worksheet 2.7

Worksheet

The Fish
W. B. Yeats

Although you hide in the ebb and flow
Of the pale tide when the moon has set,
The people of coming days will know
About the casting out of my net,
And how you have leaped times out of mind
Over the little silver cords,
And think that you were hard and unkind,
And blame you with many bitter words.

Argue: What is the text saying about the theme?

Clarify: What happens in the text to make you think this?

Confirm: What is the best example (quote)?

Extract technique: Is there a technique in the quote or elsewhere?

Scrutinise: What might the technique make the viewer *think* or *feel*?

Synthesise: How does this support what you've argued?

Worksheet 2.8

Worksheet

The Four Ages of Man
W. B. Yeats

He with body waged a fight,
but body won; it walks upright.

Then he struggled with the heart,
Innocence and peace depart.

Then he struggled with the mind,
his proud heart he left behind.

Now his wars on God begin,
At stroke of midnight God shall win.

Argue: What is the text saying about the theme?

Clarify: What happens in the text to make you think this?

Confirm: What is the best example (quote)?

Extract technique: Is there a technique in the quote or elsewhere?

Scrutinise: What might the technique make the viewer *think* or *feel*?

Synthesise: How does this support what you've argued?

Worksheet 2.9

Worksheet

No Man is an Island
John Donne

No man is an island,
Entire of itself,
Every man is a piece of the continent,
A part of the main.
If a clod be washed away by the sea,
Europe is the less.
As well as if a promontory were.
As well as if a manor of thy friend's
Or of thine own were.
Any man's death diminishes me,
Because I am involved in mankind.
And therefore, never send to know for whom the bell tolls.
It tolls for thee.

Argue: What is the text saying about the theme?

Clarify: What happens in the text to make you think this?

Confirm: What is the best example (quote)?

Extract technique: Is there a technique in the quote or elsewhere?

Scrutinise: What might the technique make the viewer *think* or *feel*?

Synthesise: How does this support what you've argued?

Worksheet 2.10

Worksheet

Love
Elizabeth Barrett Browning

We cannot live, except thus mutually
We alternate, aware or unaware,
The reflex act of life: and when we bare
Our virtue onward most impulsively,
Most full of invocation, and to be
Most instantly compellent, certes, there
We live most life, whoever breathes most air
And counts his dying years by sun and sea.
But when a soul, by choice and conscience, doth
Throw out her full force on another soul,
The conscience and the concentration both
Make mere life, Love. For Life in perfect whole
And aim consummated, is Love in sooth,
As nature's magnet-heat rounds pole with pole.

Argue: What is the text saying about the theme?

Clarify: What happens in the text to make you think this?

Confirm: What is the best example (quote)?

Extract technique: Is there a technique in the quote or elsewhere?

Scrutinise: What might the technique make the viewer *think* or *feel*?

Synthesise: How does this support what you've argued?

Worksheet 2.11

> **TIP**
>
> The micro fictions all contain irony.
>
> Irony is often difficult for students to spot. If you would like to bring their attention to it, you can try the following:
>
> Ask them to read the first two paragraphs only, stop, then fill in the Text + Theme schema in pencil. Once they've done this, have them read the remainder of the story and see if their evaluation has changed. You can then draw their attention to the fact that the ending was the opposite of what they expected, and that this is ironic.

So far, we have covered ways to analyse a text and get the analysis down on paper. We have also covered basic English essay structure and paragraph structure. We have also had some opportunities to write some generic body paragraphs.

In the next chapter we will examine essay topics and questions for English texts and how students can use these topics and questions to plan an essay using scaffolds for body paragraphs.

References

Ehren, B. J. (2002). Speech-language pathologists contributing significantly to the academic success of high school students: A vision for professional growth. *Topics in Language Disorders*, *22*(2), 60–80. https://doi.org/10.1097/00011363-200201000-00005

Kellogg, R. T. (2008). Training writing skills: A cognitive development perspective. *Journal of Writing Research*, *1*(1), 1–26.

3 Essay Topic Breakdown and Planning

> Did You Know...
> Graphic organisers, also known as concept maps and knowledge maps (Nesbit & Adesope, 2006), can improve understanding of complicated processes and tasks because they can provide visual representations of the processes involved in completing tasks. Students benefit from having tasks simplified, and from having steps to guide analysis (Santangelo et al., 2007).

Simply being presented with an essay topic can be intimidating. Just the thought of planning and writing an essay can send some students into panic. This section will provide strategies for breaking down an essay topic to make planning and writing easier.

There appear to be four basic essay topic types, and if a student can identify which type—or combination of types—they have, then this makes it easier to break topics down to plan and write their essay.

There are some grammar lessons sprinkled in this chapter where needed. Breaking down essay topics provides another opportunity to practice reading comprehension at word, sentence and paragraph level, so don't let that goal escape you.

For the purpose of this section, there are three basic sentence functions students should look out for. Each sentence in an essay question or topic will do one of the following.

Inform
Instruct
Ask

Sentences that <u>inform</u> simply supply information and don't ask or tell you to do anything:

The play, Hamlet, is a tragedy.

Sentences that <u>instruct</u>, or instructions, don't simply give you information, but tell you what to do, like an order. These sentences will start with a verb and end with a full stop:

Plot Hamlet's behaviours in the play to show his compulsive indecision.

DOI: 10.4324/9781003263401-4

Sentences that <u>ask</u> you something, you'll know. These sentences are distinct from those that inform or instruct because they're concluded with a question mark:

How does Hamlet explore the nature of indecision?

All sorts of conversation can spring from the activity in Worksheet 3.1. Students will find in both examples that the inform sentence type is used most. They might also notice that the ask sentence types (questions) will most likely appear in the novel through dialogue or as rhetorical questions. Instruct type sentences are more likely to be found in a textbook, in an activity. Ultimately, we want students to be able to tell the difference between the three types.

When students get an essay topic, they're asked to read the question carefully and underline key words. These are necessary first steps. The steps ensure that students don't mis-read the question and that they identify function words and unfamiliar words. But we're going to take this process a step further.

Remember our ACCESS scaffold for the body paragraph? In the last chapter we used the word ACCESS as an acrostic for questions that take students through the components of the body paragraph. For the 'A' question, 'Argue,' we used the question from the Text + Theme scaffold: *What is the text saying about the theme?* Answering this generic question gives students a point about the text to argue and from there they can follow through by answering the remaining questions. But what happens when they have an essay topic that is not specifically asking them to discuss the themes in the text?

As we know, the average high school English essay usually has at least three body paragraphs, yet, so far, we have a single set of questions on one scaffold. And you're correct in thinking that if students answer the same questions for all body paragraphs, then all body paragraphs will read the same. We don't want this, so students need to break down the essay topic carefully. And if they do this as outlined, they can create distinct body paragraphs while answering the same set of ACCESS questions each time.

Figure 3.1 is the adjusted body paragraph scaffold we will start with.

In figure 3.1, you've probably noticed that our Argue question has gone. This is because we will replace it with another question that directly addresses an essay topic. Again, you might be wondering if students can do this and still have three to four distinct paragraphs. They can if they use the following strategies.

Basic 'One Way' Strategy

Use this strategy for questions or topics that consist of one, maybe two, simple sentences like the one here:

How does Shakespeare's *Romeo and Juliet* explore the theme of love?

This topic question might seem straightforward to some, but for others it might be challenging to answer in essay form and so we are going to make it easier by altering some parts so it fits into our ACCESS paragraph scaffold.

After students read the question carefully, and define any unknown vocabulary, they can sharpen the question by eliminating excess words:

How does <u>Shakespeare's</u> *Romeo and Juliet* explore <u>the theme of</u> love?

Worksheet: Sentence Functions

1. Find two pages of text; one from a novel, and one from a textbook.

2. Identify the function of each sentence as either **informing**, **instructing**, or **asking**. Use three different coloured pencils, pens or highlighters for each one. Start by colour-coding the sentences functions below, so you know which one is which.

3. Count each colour.

Which sentence function is the most popular in the page from the novel?_____

Which sentence function is the most popular in the page from the textbook?_____

Sentence Functions

Sentences that <u>inform</u> simply supply information and don't ask or tell you to do anything:

The play Hamlet by William Shakespeare is a tragedy.

Sentences that <u>instruct</u>, or instructions, don't simply give you information, but tell you what to do, like an order. These sentences will start with a doing verb and end with a full stop:

Plot Hamlet's behaviour in the play to show his compulsive indecision.

Sentences that <u>ask</u> you something, you'll know. These sentences are distinct from those that inform or instruct because they are concluded with a question mark (?):

How does Hamlet explore the nature of indecision?

Worksheet 3.1

Argue:
Clarify: What happens in the text to make you think this?
Confirm: What is the best example (quote)?
Extract technique: Is there a technique in the quote or elsewhere?
Scrutinise: What might the technique make the viewer *think* or *feel*?
Synthesise: How does this support what you've argued?

Figure 3.1

So now we have. . .

How does *Romeo and Juliet* explore love?

It isn't essential that students do this last task but simplifying the question makes for some bite-sized grammar work. Next, students can shape this question in a way that allows them to answer it multiple times and in different ways.

Again, we are still working on the body paragraph. This is because body paragraphs argue the main points—they're the meat in the sandwich. They're also the most challenging parts of the essay. This is why they should be addressed first and that's why I'm leaving the introduction and conclusion for the end.

Now, I'm going to have a go at turning this essay question into an Argue question. Refer to figure 3.2.

By doing this, students create an opportunity to split responses to the essay topic into parts: They can look at 'one' way of exploring love in one paragraph, and 'one' other way in the next paragraph, and so on. Students can answer that Argue question and argue their positions. Answer it twice and students have two points, answer it three times and they have three points, and so on.

There are several ways students can start the Argue question using the basic 'one way' strategy (figure 3.3).

Argue: **What is one way** 'Romeo and Juliet' explores love?
Clarify: What happens in the text to make you think this?
Confirm: What is the best example (quote)?
Extract technique: Is there a technique in the quote or elsewhere?
Scrutinise: What might the technique make the viewer *think* or *feel*?
Synthesise: How does this support what you've argued?

Figure 3.2

Argue: What is one way...
reason...
situation...
aspect...
element...
character...
thing...

Figure 3.3

Students can add to the list in figure 3.3 and alter it as needed. Here is another example. In figure 3.4 we have transformed the essay topic into a question:
Explore why Hamlet delays killing Claudius in the play *Hamlet*.

> **TIP**
>
> If students are not sure where to start, they can look for interrogatives like 'how' and 'why.' 'Why' indicates they might start their Argue question with 'what is one *reason*,' and 'how' indicates they could use 'what is one *way*.'

Argue: **What is one reason** Hamlet delays killing Claudius?
Clarify: What happens in the text to make you think this?
Confirm: What is the best example (quote)?
Extract technique: Is there a technique in the quote or elsewhere?
Scrutinise: What might the technique make the viewer *think* or *feel*?
Synthesise: How does this support what you've argued?

Figure 3.4

Argue: What is one reason Hamlet delays killing Claudius?

Answer 1:
The first time Hamlet delays killing Claudius, he is questioning whether his father's ghost is real or imagined.

Answer 2:
Another reason Hamlet delays killing Claudius is because he gets too tied-up in his own thoughts and over-analyses.

Answer 3:
Hamlet also delays the murder of Claudius because the evidence he gathers never seems to be enough.

Figure 3.5

See figure 3.5 for an example of how it might look if we answered our Hamlet Argue question multiple times.

Depending on the text, some students might go on to answer this question a few more times. Each time students answer this question, they have one more topic sentence for a body paragraph.

You can use Worksheet 3.2 for teaching and practice. Teachers might like to apply the scaffold to essay topics for the current class text, and speech

Worksheet: Essay Topics-Basic Strategy

Below is a list of basic essay topics. See if you can convert each one into an 'Argue' guiding question. Remember, you do not have to answer any of these questions, so knowing the text isn't essential. Just re-write them as questions starting with *What is one...*

The first one has been done for you.

1) ~~Explain what makes the novel, Coraline, a gothic novel.~~ ✓

2) What sorts of themes are explored in the picture book The Rabbits?

3) With reference to The Giver, explore how a utopian society controls it citizens.

4) How does the novel Huckleberry Finn explore prejudice?

5) In Othello, which key incidents bring about Othello's downfall?

6) Which elements of Macbeth make the play a tragedy?

1 **Argue:** What is one *thing that makes Coraline a gothic novel?* ✓
   Clarify: What happens in the text to make you think this?

2 **Argue:** What is one
   Clarify: What happens in the text to make you think this?

3 **Argue:** What is one
   Clarify: What happens in the text to make you think this?

4 **Argue:** What is one
   Clarify: What happens in the text to make you think this?

5 **Argue:** What is one
   Clarify: What happens in the text to make you think this?

6 **Argue:** What is one
   Clarify: What happens in the text to make you think this?

Worksheet 3.2

pathologists might ask the student or classroom teacher for relevant essay topics to use for practice. For data collection, you might even revisit the worksheet to check progress after a reasonable period of practise or even keep the worksheet aside to monitor for improvements and check progress so you can make any necessary adjustments or move on to the next goal or target.

Agree/Disagree Strategy

The next strategy is for essay topics that require students to agree or disagree.

We will still use 'What is one. . .' to start our steering questions, but we have more steps to get there because these topics are usually made up of more than one sentence. To start with, we'll take another look at verbs.

Previously we looked at doing and being verbs. For students, being verbs are words like is, are, am, was and were. They might understand that doing verbs are words like running, looked, catch and so on. But there's a few more for them to get through.

We know that the words in figure 3.6 are also verbs—modal and auxiliary verbs. Students might like to know that they can be found crowded around other verbs in a sentence. For the purposes of our strategy, we can also label these 'helper' verbs, telling students that these words help the main verb.

Here are some examples you can share with students of these verbs working with other verbs:

She <u>can run</u> faster than her friends.
It <u>could be farther</u> than we thought.
He <u>might have gotten</u> home on time if he hadn't missed the bus.

You could let students know that these are 'verb phrases,' and they can be made up of one verb or many. They usually include words like adverbs too, but

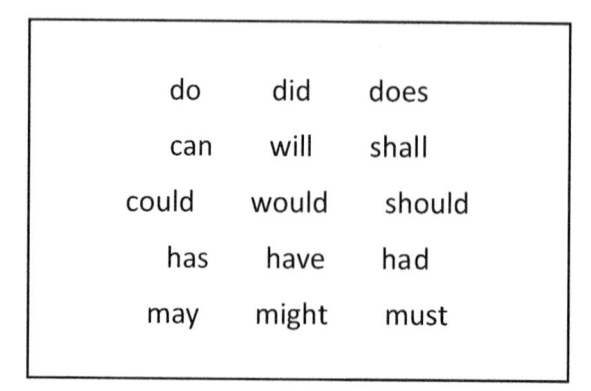

do	did	does
can	will	shall
could	would	should
has	have	had
may	might	must

Figure 3.6

adverbs can clutter sentences, so we won't worry too much about these. We will just concentrate on finding these verb clusters.

You could work through the following examples with your students underlining the verb phrases in the sentences. This might be an activity students can do in pairs after learning about these verbs and seeing the earlier examples. Professionals working one-to-one with students might do the first couple with the student.

> *We might have been waiting forever.*
> *I will call you next time.*
> *He can drive the car to the shops.*
> *You could be driving for a long time.*
> *It will be easier on all of us.*
> *I shall let you know as soon as the package arrives.*

Next, you could work though negatives and discuss how they can accompany verbs to indicate what something is *not* being or doing (figures 3.7 and 3.8). Students can learn that negatives can be placed into the verb phrase to express the opposite. Next are some examples you can use.

> *They never wanted this to happen.*
> *It was not in her best interest to attend the event.*
> *People could never understand why he was so successful.*

Sometimes students will have to add *do, does* and *did* to the word *not*.

> *It seems fair to keep all of the students in detention after school.*
> *I expect less of Ben.*
> *She ran across the road.*

```
┌─────────────────────────────────┐
│                                 │
│         not       never         │
│                                 │
└─────────────────────────────────┘
```

Figure 3.7

```
┌─────────────────────────────────┐
│                                 │
│    do not    does not    did not│
│                                 │
└─────────────────────────────────┘
```

Figure 3.8

These can be altered in the following way as an example:

> It <u>does not seem</u> fair to keep all the students in detention after school.
> I <u>do not expect</u> less of Ben.
> She <u>did not run</u> across the road.

> **TIP**
>
> For the verbs do, does and did, make sure students remember they might have to alter the main verb tense. They can say the sentences aloud and listen to see if the verb sounds right or needs changing.

For the agree/disagree strategy students can follow the process for the basic 'One Way' Strategy. They can use the same template but keep or alter the verbs depending on whether they agree or disagree with the statements presented.

The structure of agree/disagree essay topics frequently follows a sentence pattern:
Inform sentence type. Instruct sentence type.
Or
Inform sentence type. Ask sentence type.

Students might find it helpful to identify the inform sentence, the statement. This is the sentence students will either agree or disagree with. Worksheet 3.3 has only inform type sentences. Students can use these to practice negation using not, never, do not, does not, and did not.

Worksheet 3.4 is an opportunity for students to practice identifying the inform sentence and then create a negative statement (or not). Students can then apply the basic 'one way' Strategy from the first section of this chapter to complete the Argue section at the start of the body paragraphs provided.

Pronouns

Before we move on to the next strategy, we have another grammar lesson for students. This one is to do with pronouns. There's a few in figure 3.9.

You could explain to students that pronouns are those short, simple words we use in place of nouns. They help point to who and what and save us from repeating ourselves:

> Alice likes to dance. <u>She</u> can dance all night!

It might be helpful to point out to students that pronouns can confuse, so must be used carefully:

> Ben and Oliver hate dancing. <u>He</u> avoids it whenever he can!

Worksheet: Insert Negatives

| not | never | do not | does not | did not |

1) Underline the <u>verbs</u> in the sentences below.

2) Turn them into negatives by choosing one of the options from the box. The first three have been done for you.

Some people *never*^ <u>learn</u> to cope with stress.

War *not*^ <u>is</u> a game.

Rebecca *does not*^ <u>likes</u> salad.

The most popular books are always the best books.

Watching movies all the time is good for you.

I think there are many bad people in the world.

You should talk with your mouth full of food.

You can tell how nice a person is by the way they look.

He stomped mud through the house.

He was going to put the milk away.

They go to the markets every Saturday.

She would have gone out without her jacket if she knew it was raining.

Worksheet 3.3

Worksheet: Agree/Disagree Strategy

Work through the following essay topics. We ordinarily might agree with the following statements. However, try disagreeing so you get a chance to practise what you've learned.

✓ 1) Great literature can transform how you view the world. To what extent do you agree with this statement?

2) Ambition is destructive. Explain why you agree or disagree with close reference to Macbeth.

3) The novel Trash is a rags-to-riches story like the film Slumdog Millionaire. Agree or disagree and explain why?

4) The Happiest Refugee is a story about courage. Do you agree or disagree with this?

5) The effects of war endure long after a war is over. With reference to Maus, decide how much you agree or disagree with this statement.

6) Sooner or later the truth will come out. How true is this statement? Answer with close reference to Shoehorn Sonata.

1 Argue: What is one *reason why great literature can not transform how we view the world?* ✓
   Clarify: What happens in the text to make you think this?

2 Argue: What is one
   Clarify: What happens in the text to make you think this?

3 Argue: What is one
   Clarify: What happens in the text to make you think this?

4 Argue: What is one
   Clarify: What happens in the text to make you think this?

5 Argue: What is one
   Clarify: What happens in the text to make you think this?

6 Argue: What is one
   Clarify: What happens in the text to make you think this?

Worksheet 3.4

Essay Topic Breakdown and Planning 77

```
┌─────────────────────────────────┐
│     I   he   she   they   it    │
│                                 │
│    me   him   her   them   it   │
│                                 │
│           this   that           │
└─────────────────────────────────┘
```

Figure 3.9

Romeo and Juliet explores (different kinds of love.) How does the text explore (this?)

Figure 3.10

Students can see that the last example is confusing because we aren't sure whether 'he' is referring to Ben or Oliver.

In essay topics with more than one sentence, students will see pronouns that refer to nouns in previous sentences. Sometimes, they might want to substitute the pronoun for the full noun phrase to clear up confusion. Take the example in figure 3.10, where I've circled the noun phrase and pronoun.

This might become:
How does the text explore <u>different kinds of love</u>?
If we turn this into a basic 'one way' question, then it becomes:
<u>What is one way</u> the text explores <u>different kinds of love</u>?
Students could also go as far as replacing 'the text' with 'Romeo and Juliet' if they like. Point is, identifying pronouns helps condense the topic. Especially if students have a two-sentence essay topic: an inform sentence followed by an ask or instruct sentence type.

See the Appendix for a full list of pronouns. You can even supply this list to your students or make it visible in the classroom or clinic. Worksheet 3.5 has a few examples for student practice.

Divide and Conquer Strategy

For this strategy students will look for groups within essay topics, groups of things in threes and fours. Instead of a single 'what is one. . .' question we will make a distinct and separate Argue steering question for each paragraph.

Take the following example from *Othello*:
Desdemona and Othello's relationship is beset by obstacles from the start. How does social status, age, and race pose problems for this couple in the play, *Othello*?

This example contains two sentences: one informs and one asks. The inform sentence provides additional information to clarify the question, so the 'ask' sentence type, our question, will be the focus.

Worksheet: Text, Theme, Genre

1) identify the pronouns below and what they refer to (circle and link)

Romeo and Juliet explores different kinds of love. How does the text explore this?

2) Re-word the sentences into 'What is one...' guiding questions.

Shoe-Horn Sonata features brave women. How does the text show they were as brave as the men?

What is one... _____

_____

_____

Some children's stories explore very dark topics. Is Alice in Wonderland one of them?

What is one... _____

_____

_____

In The Lord of the Flies, the conch is central in showing the boy's gradual decent into depravity. How does it show this?

What is one... _____

_____

_____

Worksheet 3.5

I have identified a pattern of three as well: "social status, age, and race." I have also identified what the pronoun in "this couple" is referring to so I can replace it with "Othello and Desdemona."

Now I have this figured out, I can rewrite the topic to plan for a three-body paragraph essay in figure 3.11.

You might use the following example of an essay topic based on *To Kill a Mockingbird* by Harper Lee (1960):

Racism is a central theme in *To Kill a Mockingbird*. How does the portrayal of characters in the novel, like Calpurnia, Tom, and the African American community, explore this topic?

Firstly, you might assist students to identify three aspects they can talk about separately: like Calpurnia, Tom, and the African American community.

Next, you might help students to identify that the pronoun used in "this theme?" refers to "racism" in the previous sentence, so they can substitute the phrase and not have to worry about the first sentence. The essay topic might look a bit like figure 3.12 by now.

If students rewrite the topic, simplifying it to a single sentence, it might look something like this:

How does the portrayal of characters in the novel, like Calpurnia, Tom, and the African American community, explore racism?

Now, students can break this into three separate questions. Figure 3.13 shows what our three Argue questions might look like for the *To Kill a Mockingbird* essay topic.

Word	Definition
obstacle	*Something that gets in the way or creates problems.*
Word	Definition
beset	*To be surrounded by something*
Argue 1 thing	*How does social status create problems for Othello and Desdemona's relationship?*
Argue 2nd thing	*How does age create obstacles for Othello and Desdemona's relationship?*
Argue 3rd thing	*How does race create problems for Othello and Desdemona's relationship?*
Argue 4th thing (optional)	

Figure 3.11

Racism is a central theme in To Kill a Mockingbird. How does the portrayal of characters in the novel, like Calpurnia, Tom, and the African American community, explore this theme?

(Racism is circled; "Calpurnia, Tom, and the African American community" is underlined; "portrayal" is circled/marked.)

Figure 3.12

Word	Definition
portrayal	*The way something is shown—like a description*
Word	Definition
Argue 1 thing	*How does the portrayal of Calpurnia explore racism?*
Argue 2nd thing	*How does the portrayal of Tom explore racism?*
Argue 3rd thing	*How does the portrayal of The African American community explore racism?*
Argue 4th thing (optional)	

Figure 3.13

See Worksheets 3.6 to 3.8 for practice items and blank scaffolds based on the following essay topics:

1) *The Rabbits* is an allegorical tale of Australian Colonisation. In what ways does the setting, and the use of rabbits and possums, show this?
2) *Burial Rites* features the vulnerable in society. How does Hannah Kent's narrative evoke sympathy for the plight of women, the impoverished, and convicted criminals?
3) "Love conquers all." How do the characters Oberon, Hermia, and one other character in *A Midsummer Night's Dream* demonstrate this idea?
4) *The Lord of the Flies* depicts the human capacity for violence. Discuss, choosing three key scenes which examine this.

Worksheet: Divide & Conquer

Try breaking up the following essay topics into smaller questions by applying the Divide and Conquer strategy. Find three to four things. If you feel confident, you might want to try to substitute the pronouns too.

1) The Rabbits is an allegorical tale of Australian Colonisation. In what ways does the setting, and the use of rabbits and possums show this?

2) Burial Rites features the vulnerable in society. How does Hannah Kent's narrative evoke sympathy for the plight of women, the impoverished, and convicted criminals?

3) "love conquers all." How do the characters Oberon, Hermia, and one other character in A Midsummer Night's Dream demonstrate this idea?

4) The Lord of the Flies depicts the human capacity for violence. Discuss, choosing three key scenes which examine this.

5) How does language work to keep society under control in The Giver? Choose three or four words (like released, newchildren, climate control, and elsewhere) and explain how they are used to do this.

6) Hamlet is a revenge story, but it is also a story of loyalty, equivocation and distrust. How might the text explore these different themes?

1

Word	Definition
Word	Definition
Argue 1 thing	
Argue 2nd thing	
Argue 3rd thing	
Argue 4th thing (optional)	

Worksheet 3.6

82 *Essay Topic Breakdown and Planning*

2

Word	Definition
Word	Definition
Argue 1 thing	
Argue 2nd thing	
Argue 3rd thing	

3

Word	Definition
Word	Definition
Argue 1 thing	
Argue 2nd thing	
Argue 3rd thing	

4

Word	Definition
Word	Definition
Argue 1 thing	
Argue 2nd thing	
Argue 3rd thing	

Worksheet 3.7

Essay Topic Breakdown and Planning 83

5

Word	Definition
Word	Definition
Argue 1 thing	
Argue 2nd thing	
Argue 3rd thing	
Argue 4th thing (optional)	

6

Word	Definition
Word	Definition
Argue 1 thing	
Argue 2nd thing	
Argue 3rd thing	
Argue 4th thing (optional)	

Worksheet 3.8

5) How does language work to keep society under control in *The Giver*? Choose three or four words (like released, newchildren, climate control, and elsewhere) and explain how they are used to do this.
6) *Hamlet* is a revenge story, but it is also a story of loyalty, equivocation and distrust. How might the text explore these different themes?

Incorporate Strategy

Longer essay topics, with multiple sentences, can be confusing for students with language and learning disabilities. Often the question or instruction is buried in a paragraph of information. But once the instruction or question is identified, students can apply the strategies we have covered so far. Other times though, instructions will be littered around multiple sentences and prove a chore to locate.

This strategy is for longer topics, topics that ask about themes, characters, scenes and plots but also ask you to explain things, discuss techniques and other elements that are already covered by the ACCESS scaffold.

Take the following example:

Can crossing boundaries benefit people? Answer with reference to *Maestro* by Peter Goldsworthy. Explain your reasoning and show how literary techniques are used to highlight this theme in the text.

Students might approach this question by starting with the first strategy and working through subsequent strategies: It's not a single sentence or short essay topic, so our basic strategy won't apply. It isn't an agree/disagree question, and there isn't anything clearly in three's or four's that we can divide between our body paragraphs. So, let's look at what we do have.

We do have some key words that link to our ACCESS scaffold areas. I've circled them in figure 3.14. using the essay topic on *Maestro* by Peter Goldsworthy (2014).

To recap, figure 3.15 shows the ACCESS paragraph scaffold with our steering questions. As you can see there is a steering question that asks us to explain or 'clarify' our reasoning and questions that address literary techniques. Check the Appendix for *Incorporate Strategy Vocabulary Sheet* for a list of words students can look for, to see which of the ACCESS sections they apply to.

In this case, students can take the components of the question that fit into these other parts of the ACCESS scaffold, then reshape or highlight those

Can crossing boundaries benefit people? Answer with reference to Maestro by Peter Goldsworthy. Explain your reasoning and show how literary techniques are used to highlight this theme in the text.

Figure 3.14

Argue:
Clarify: What happens in the text to make you think this?
Confirm: What is the best example (quote)?
Extract technique: Is there a technique in the quote or elsewhere?
Scrutinise: What might the technique make the viewer *think* or *feel*?
Synthesise: How does this support what you've argued?

Figure 3.15

Argue:
Clarify: What happens in the text to make you think this?
Confirm: What is the best example (quote)?
Extract technique: Is there a technique in the quote or elsewhere?
Scrutinise: What might the technique make the viewer *think* or *feel*?
Synthesise: How does this support what you've argued?

Figure 3.16

> **A**rgue: What is one *way crossing boundaries benefits people in Maestro?*
>
> **C**larify: What happens in the text to make you think this?

Figure 3.17

sections of the scaffold accordingly. Then, they can just take them out of the essay topic altogether.

Can crossing boundaries benefit people? Answer with reference to *Maestro* by Peter Goldsworthy. Explain your reasoning and show how literary techniques are used to highlight this theme in the text.

Now, we are left with:

Can crossing boundaries benefit people? Answer with reference to *Maestro* by Peter Goldsworthy.

Students now have something they can convert into a basic 'one way' question. Students can decide whether crossing boundaries benefits people or not in the text, and then write an Argue question.

Students can practice this strategy using Worksheets 3.9–3.11 using the following essay topics.

1) In Shakespeare's play, Othello's fatal flaw is jealousy. How does the play explore jealousy as a theme, and which techniques are used to illuminate this theme in the play?
2) Wilfred Owen's war poems are vivid in their description of the lived experience of war and young life lost. Examine how Owen uses language to communicate the horror of war with close reference to at least two of his poems.
3) What is *The Taming of the Shrew* saying about women? Identify techniques which best exemplify this and explain how they do this.
4) The picture book, *The Arrival* by Shaun Tan uses no words, only pictures. How effective is this method of storytelling in getting across the story of migration and new beginnings? Refer to specific visual techniques to support your response.
5) It is in times of crisis that people show their true colours. How does this idea apply to the characters in *The Sky So Heavy*? Explain your answer with close reference to the text and its language.
6) *Coraline* is filled with symbolism and imagery. How does symbolism and imagery make *Coraline* a gothic novel?

Worksheet: Incorporate Strategy

Using the essay topics below, try to practise the incorporate strategy. Apply the topics below to the relevant sections on the blank ACCESS scaffolds provided. Don't forget, you don't have to answer these questions here, just formulate them.

Use the vocabulary sheet to help identify paragraph sections in the topics below.

1) In Shakespeare's play, Othello's fatal flaw is jealousy. How does the play explore jealousy as a theme, and which techniques are used to illuminate this theme in the play?

2) Wilfred Owen's war poems are vivid in their description of the lived experience of war and young life lost. Examine how Owen uses language to communicate the horror of war with close reference to at least two of his poems.

3) What is The Taming of the Shrew saying about women? Identify techniques which best exemplify this and explain how they do this.

4) The picture book, The Arrival by Shaun Tan uses no words, only pictures. How effective is this method of storytelling in getting across the story of migration and new beginnings? Refer to specific visual techniques to support your response.

5) It is in times of crisis that people show their true colours. How does this idea apply to the characters in The Sky So Heavy? Explain your answer with close reference to the text and its language.

6) Coraline is filled with symbolism and imagery. How does symbolism and imagery make Coraline a gothic novel?

1
Argue: What is one
Clarify: What happens in the text to make you think this?
Confirm: What is the best example (quote)?
Extract technique: Is there a technique in the quote or elsewhere?
Scrutinise: What might the technique make the viewer *think* or *feel*?
Synthesise: How does this support what you've argued?

Worksheet 3.9

88 *Essay Topic Breakdown and Planning*

2 Argue: What is one

Clarify: What happens in the text to make you think this?

Confirm: What is the best example (quote)?

Extract technique: Is there a technique in the quote or elsewhere?

Scrutinise: What might the technique make the viewer *think* or *feel*?

Synthesise: How does this support what you've argued?

3 Argue: What is one

Clarify: What happens in the text to make you think this?

Confirm: What is the best example (quote)?

Extract technique: Is there a technique in the quote or elsewhere?

Scrutinise: What might the technique make the viewer *think* or *feel*?

Synthesise: How does this support what you've argued?

4 Argue: What is one

Clarify: What happens in the text to make you think this?

Confirm: What is the best example (quote)?

Extract technique: Is there a technique in the quote or elsewhere?

Scrutinise: What might the technique make the viewer *think* or *feel*?

Synthesise: How does this support what you've argued?

Worksheet 3.10

Essay Topic Breakdown and Planning 89

5	**A**rgue: What is one
	Clarify: What happens in the text to make you think this?
	Confirm: What is the best example (quote)?
	Extract technique: Is there a technique in the quote or elsewhere?
	Scrutinise: What might the technique make the viewer *think* or *feel*?
	Synthesise: How does this support what you've argued?

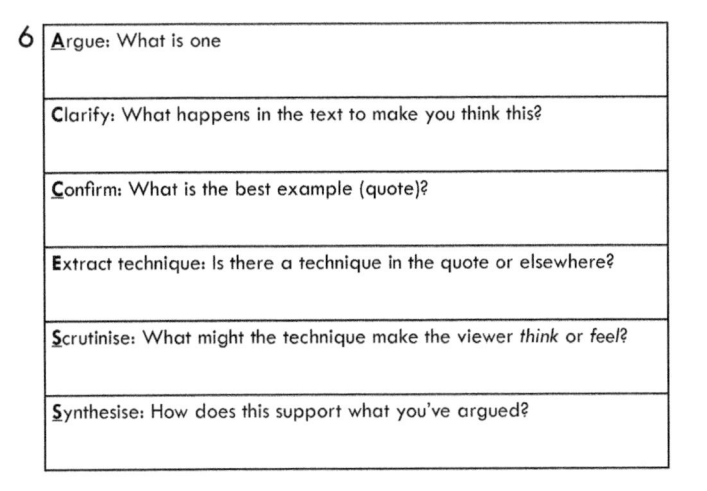

6	**A**rgue: What is one
	Clarify: What happens in the text to make you think this?
	Confirm: What is the best example (quote)?
	Extract technique: Is there a technique in the quote or elsewhere?
	Scrutinise: What might the technique make the viewer *think* or *feel*?
	Synthesise: How does this support what you've argued?

Worksheet 3.11

Students now have four strategies to apply to breaking down essay topics. Next, teachers and speech pathologists might like to collect some essay topics and questions on the current prescribed text and see if students can apply the strategies to plan their arguments.

References

Goldsworthy, P. (2014). *Maestro* (5th ed.). HarperCollins Australia.

Lee, H. (1960). *To kill a mockingbird*. Vintage.

Nesbit, J. C., & Adesope, O. O. (2006). Learning with concept and knowledge maps: A meta-analysis. *Review of Educational Research*, 76(3), 413–448. https://doi.org/10.3102/00346543076003413

Santangelo, T. H., Karen, R., & Graham, S. (2007). Self-regulated strategy development: A validated model to support students who struggle with writing. *Learning Disabilities: A Contemporary Journal*, 5(1), 1–20.

4 Writing an English Essay

> Did You Know...
> In a meta-analysis of instructional practices to improve adolescent writing skills, Graham and Perin (2007) found that instructions teaching specific strategies for planning and revising proved to be the most effective strategies of the instructions reviewed.

Let's recap! We've covered ways of analysing texts through identifying themes and making comments about them. We've looked at the overall structure of an essay, and the structure of a body paragraph for an English essay. We've learnt how to use questions to steer students through writing paragraphs, and four strategies for breaking down essay topics and for adjusting our paragraph scaffold to suit them.

In this section we will bring it all together by demonstrating how students can practise planning and writing introductions, conclusions and entire essays.

Introductions

We know that introductions tell the reader what the essay is about; they say what the writer is about to say. In essays, it's much easier for students to summarise the arguments they've made after they've already been made, and that's why I've left this component until last.

We've already applied questions to help students to plan and write body paragraphs, so we'll continue along these lines by following some steering questions for introductions as well. Our introduction scaffold is figure 4.1. To remember the questions students can use the acronym PREP.

The paraphrase section is optional, and it asks students to produce a 'fluffy first' sentence. Here, students can reword the essay question. Competent essay writers won't usually do this, but for students who struggle it's a handy way to get going.

Paraphrase: What's your fluffy first sentence? (OPTIONAL)
Respond: What is your short answer/response to the essay topic?
Explain: Are there any terms you need to define for your reader? (OPTIONAL)
Points: What are your body paragraph Arguments?

Figure 4.1

Paraphrase: What's your fluffy first sentence? (OPTIONAL)   *There are a few reasons why Hamlet delays killing Claudius in Shakespeare's play.*
Respond: What is your short answer/response to the essay topic?   *Hamlet has a problem with taking action and seems to find excuses for delaying his decision.*
Explain: Are there any terms you need to define for your reader? (OPTIONAL)
Points: What are your body paragraph Arguments?   *Hamlet delays because he thinks he might be imagining his father's ghost. He also over-analyses which wastes time, and he never seems satisfied with the proof he uncovers.*

Figure 4.2

There are a few reasons why Hamlet delays killing Claudius in Shakespeare's play. Hamlet has a problem with taking action and seems to find excuses for delaying his decision. Hamlet delays because he thinks he might be imagining his father's ghost. He also over-analyses which wastes time, and he never seems satisfied with the proof he uncovers.

Figure 4.3

After students have written their fluffy first sentence, they'll need to respond directly to the essay topic. This is where they write their general answer or response to the topic.

In the following section, students can explain to their readers anything that might support or make their argument clearer. They might like to define some terms, and if students are writing about more than one text, they can name these here.

As we know, students must include body paragraph points in their introduction. They can even go as far as to copy each argument or Argue answer verbatim, which is the first sentence of each body paragraph. They will go in the final Points section.

We might take one of our previous essay topics to demonstrate how this works. Since we already have three body paragraph points for the *Hamlet* essay topic from Chapter 3, we will apply it to the introduction PREP scaffold (see figure 4.2).

Explore why Hamlet delays killing Claudius in the play *Hamlet*.

When the scaffold is taken away, (see figure 4.3) what's left over is an introduction to the essay.

This is light and short, I know, but it does the job an introduction needs to do. Students can practice formulating introductions using the paragraphs they developed from the activities at the end of Chapter 2.

Conclusions

Conclusions are funny things. They're not often used to great effect and usually just restate what has already been said, which makes them a little useless considering the introduction already does this.

Under exam conditions, struggling students don't get around to writing conclusions because they often run out of time. And if students do manage to write a conclusion, it often echoes the introduction, and does a better job at it—another reason why it's especially prudent to leave introductions and conclusions until last, even in exams. Conclusions generally make better introductions in most cases because students often write their introductions first, fuss over them and waste time, then if they get a chance to write the conclusion, time permitting, they have a much better idea of what their essay is about, having just finished it.

Conclusions can be brief but, if done well, are the drawstring that brings an argument to a close. To make the most of students' conclusions, we will track back to the beginning to revise the first chapter Text + Theme schema and the ACCESS body paragraph scaffold.

When students know the ACCESS scaffold well enough, we can make a small adjustment to one section of the scaffold. See figure 4.4.

I've changed the 'synthesise' question and this change should look familiar; it's the question from our Text + Theme scaffold and the generic Argue question we use on the ACCESS scaffold from Chapter 2, for self-study when we don't have any particular essay topic to address.

This is our final version of the body paragraph scaffold, and this is the scaffold we will start with when we have an essay topic to address. This new ACCESS scaffold also helps students with their conclusions, which brings us to our conclusion scaffold. The last component to conclude an essay, is our PS scaffold where we polish and summarise in figure 4.5.

To polish, students take their short answer to the essay topic, from the introduction, and restate it. This might mean simply shortening it.

To summarise what they've synthesised, students will study their answers to all synthesise questions from their body paragraphs, then decide what it all means. For this they must ask themselves, what do all of these observations have in common? We'll look at this in more detail shortly.

Argue:
Clarify: What happens in the text to make you think this?
Confirm: What is the best example of this (quote)?
Extract technique: Which technique demonstrates this?
Scrutinise: What is the technique supposed to make the viewer *think* or *feel*?
Synthesise: ~~How does all of this support your initial assertion?~~ What is the text saying about the theme(s)?

Figure 4.4

Polish: Can you restate and refine your overall response to the topic?
Summarise what you've synthesised: What do these observations have in common? *Ultimately, the text shows…*

Figure 4.5

This process will build students' skills in deciding what the text is saying about the theme, and also support students with language and learning difficulties to squeeze a little more depth from the text, to sum up with a meaningful conclusion that is more than just a tacked-on necessity.

Putting It All Together

I will now demonstrate how we can put the whole essay together. Students will take information from complete body paragraphs to formulate their introduction and conclusion. I'll continue this demonstration in the order I suggest students follow, starting with the body paragraphs, followed by the introduction, then the conclusion. Finally, I will show you what the complete essay should look like once we have removed the scaffolds. To start with, we'll revisit an essay topic from Chapter 3:

With reference to *The Giver*, explore how a utopian society controls its citizens.

Students might want to define 'utopian.'

utopian/utopia

A society that is supposed to be perfect and blissful.

Now that we have recapped our definition, let's apply a strategy to break down the topic. The topic's only short, it's not asking students to agree or disagree, and it's not asking them to address a range of things (so we don't need to decide if we have three's and four's) and it's not asking about anything that's already incorporated in the ACCESS scaffold. Therefore, we can apply a basic 'one way' strategy to plan this essay:

In *The Giver*, <u>what is one way</u> the utopian society controls its citizens?

Now we have a question we can answer multiple times, we can place this in the body paragraph scaffold (see figure 4.6).

Next, I'll answer this question, making sure my response is different each time, then go on to answer the other questions in the paragraph scaffold (see figures 4.7 to 4.9).

Then we complete our PREP Introduction Scaffold (figure 4.10).

Argue: *In The Giver, what is one way the utopian society controls its citizens?*
Clarify: What happens in the text to make you think this?
Confirm: What is the best example (quote)?
Extract technique: Is there a technique in the quote or elsewhere?
Scrutinise: What might the technique make the viewer *think* or *feel*?
Synthesise: What is the text saying about the theme(s)?

Figure 4.6

For my PS Conclusion scaffold, I will place all of the answers to my body paragraph 'synthesise' questions in the table in figure 4.11. This way I can observe them all and decide what they all probably mean collectively, then write this in the summarise section of the PS, conclusion scaffold.

When the scaffolding is removed, the following is what we are left with.

Complete Essay: *The Giver*

> There are many ways that the society controls its citizens in The Giver by Lois Lowry. The Utopian society in The Giver controls its citizens through language and strict rules that dictate conduct and how people must live their lives. In The Giver, strict use of words, eliminating memories, and making everything and everyone the same are also strategies used to control.
>
> The text shows how words are used to control society. In the text, people are killed when they don't meet societal expectations, including imperfect newborns, the old. The community knows release can be used as punishment and, in this case, is shameful, but they are not aware of the truth; they think the released are sent away Elsewhere. For example, in Chapter 1, we learn

1	**Argue:** What is one way the utopian society controls its citizens? *The text shows how words are used to control society.*
	Clarify: What happens in the text to make you think this? *In the text, people are killed when they don't meet societal expectations, including imperfect newborns, and the old. The community knows Release can be used as punishment and is shameful, but they are not aware of the truth. They think the released are sent away to Elsewhere.*
	Confirm: What is the best example (quote)? *For example, in Chapter 1, we learn about "a boy in [Jonas's] group of Elevens whose father had been released years before. No one ever mentioned it."*
	Extract technique: Is there a technique in the quote or elsewhere? *The techniques used here are euphemism and irony*
	Scrutinise: What might the technique make the viewer *think* or *feel*? *The euphemism, 'Released', is ironic because it is a pleasant term for an unpleasant topic, and the reader finds this even more disturbing because they know what really happens when people are released while the community does not.*
	Synthesise: What is the text saying about the theme(s)? *This shows how language can be deceptive and dishonest and used to cover-up the true nature of things.*

Figure 4.7

about "a boy in [Jonas's] group of Elevens whose father had been released years before. No one ever mentioned it" (Lowry, 2008). The techniques used here are euphemism and irony. The euphemism, 'release,' is ironic because it is a pleasant term for an unpleasant topic, and the reader finds this even more disturbing because the reader knows what really happens when people are released, and the community does not. This shows how language can be deceptive and dishonest and used to cover up the true nature of things.

By eliminating memories, the Committee of Elders can control its citizens and stop them from engaging in harmful behaviour. In the text, memories are erased from society. This way people can't remember bad events or feel pain. Since pain can make people act out, the Committee removes the threat of negative behaviours. "Without the memories it's all meaningless" (Lowry, 2008). Here is an example of hyperbole. The hyperbole, "all", emphasises the importance of memory. It shows memory is essential, for better or worse. This shows that without memories, people cannot behave badly, but they also can't experience the happiness that memories bring.

2	**A**rgue: What is one way the utopian society controls its citizens? *By eliminating memories, the Committee of Elders can control its citizens and stop them from engaging in harmful behaviour.*
	Clarify: What happens in the text to make you think this? *In the text, memories are erased from society. Citizens can't remember bad events or feel pain. Since pain can make people act-out, the committee removes the threat of negative behaviours.*
	Confirm: What is the best example (quote)? *"Without the memories, it's all meaningless."*
	Extract technique: Is there a technique in the quote or elsewhere? *Here is an example of hyperbole.*
	Scrutinise: What might the technique make the viewer *think* or *feel*? *The hyperbole, 'all', emphasises the importance of memory. It shows memory is essential, for better or worse.*
	Synthesise: What is the text saying about the theme(s)? *This shows that without memories, people cannot behave badly, but they also can't experience the happiness that memories bring.*

Figure 4.8

Another way the society controls its citizens is by making everything and everyone the same. Citizens cannot choose who they marry or their jobs. They even see things the same way because they cannot see colour. This is used to control and limit people's freedom to make choices. For example, civilian life is described as "The life where nothing was ever unexpected. Or inconvenient. Or unusual. The life without colour, pain or past" (Lowry, 2008). The technique here is repetition. Repetition of 'The life' at the start of each sentence emphasises the parallel between a life that is unchanged and the same, and one that is uninteresting and dull. The text shows people can't discriminate if they're all the same, but it also means people can't celebrate the things that make us different, experience the joys of uniqueness, or have the right to choose.

Language and strict rules are used to control citizens in The Giver. Ultimately, the text shows there is a dual nature to the utopian community and for life to be worth living, both sides of human nature, good and bad, should be embraced.

3	**A**rgue: What is one way the utopian society controls its citizens? *Another way the society controls its citizens is by making everything and everyone the same.*
	Clarify: What happens in the text to make you think this? *Citizens cannot choose who they marry or their jobs. They even see things the same way because they cannot see colour. This is used to control and limit people's freedom to make choices.*
	Confirm: What is the best example (quote)? *For example, civilian life is described as "The life where nothing was ever unexpected. Or inconvenient. Or unusual. The life without colour, pain or past."*
	Extract technique: Is there a technique in the quote or elsewhere? *The technique here is repetition.*
	Scrutinise: What might the technique make the viewer *think* or *feel*? *Repetition of 'the life' at the start of each sentence emphasises the parallel between a life that is unchanged and the same, and one that is uninteresting and dull.*
	Synthesise: What is the text saying about the theme(s)? *The text shows people can't discriminate if they're all the same, but it also means people can't celebrate the things that make them different, experience the joys of uniqueness, or have the right to choose.*

Figure 4.9

Paraphrase: What's your fluffy first sentence? (OPTIONAL) *There are many ways that the society controls its citizens in The Giver by Lois Lowry.*
Respond: What is your short answer/response to the essay topic? *The Utopian society in The Giver controls its citizens through language and strict rules that dictate conduct and how people must live their lives*
Explain: Is there anything to clarify for your reader? definitions? etc. (OPTIONAL)
Points: What are your body paragraph Arguments? *In The Giver, strict use of words, eliminating memories, and making everything and everyone the same are specific strategies used to control.*

Figure 4.10

> **S**ynthesise 1:
> *This shows how language can be deceptive and dishonest and used to cover-up the true nature of things.*

> **S**ynthesise 2:
> *This shows that without memories, people cannot behave badly, but they also can't experience the happiness that memories bring.*

> **S**ynthesise 3:
> *The text shows people can't discriminate if they're all the same, but it also means people can't celebrate the things that make us different, experience the joys of uniqueness, or have the right to choose.*

Figure 4.11

> **P**olish: Can you restate and refine your overall response to the topic?
> *Language and strict rules are used to control citizens in The Giver.*

> **S**ummarise what you've synthesised: What do these observations have in common? Ultimately, the text shows…*there is a dual nature to the utopian community and for life to be worth living, both sides of human nature, good and bad, should be embraced.*

Figure 4.12

As you can see by comparing our scaffolds and the essay text, we have re-ordered our paragraphs to create a complete essay. From here, students can edit their final product to check that their sentences make sense and correct any spelling errors. For copies of blank scaffolds that follow the same sequence, see the Appendix.

Remember, answers can be any length students want and observations can be simple or sophisticated. The scaffolds are supposed to make writing an essay simpler. The aim is for students with language and learning difficulties to build complexity into their ideas using clear language, and to avoid any unnecessary complexity in the process that gets them there.

> **TIP**
>
> For essays on two or more texts, students can answer the body paragraph Argue question for each text: In a three body-paragraph essay that's twice for one text and once for another. In a four body-paragraph essay; that's two paragraphs on each text.

Exams

The following strategies will help students apply what they've learnt in an exam. This is especially relevant for seniors at high school, preparing for final exams, because they won't receive the essay topic beforehand.

The first step is to know which schemas, scaffolds and strategies work for each student. They must learn them off-by-heart, and get good at using them, then all they need to memorise for exams is their quotations. The following is a list of what they'll need to know well. It might be helpful to share this with students so they remember why their scaffolds and strategies are important.

The Text + Theme schemas and strategies
WHY?
To study unseen texts, and to 'synthesise' your body paragraphs.

The essay structure questions: ACCESS, PREP, and PS scaffold questions
WHY?
To plan and write your essay and stay on topic.

The 4 Essay Topic Break-down strategies
WHY?
To do what you've been asked to do, plan how you'll do it, and to stay on track, making sure you address the topic all the way to the end.

In exams, however, students will still need a place to write the ACCESS questions down, so they have a plan to follow. They'll need to get their scaffold down on a spare piece of paper to formulate the Argue question. And since they cannot take spare pieces of paper into an exam, this is where the blank page comes in.

You might explain to students that 'the blank page' is a page they might find in exam question booklets. It seems like an odd thing to place onto what is obviously an empty page, but the blank page is not an oversight. It is sometimes placed in exam booklets so students have a spare piece of paper, separate from the answer booklet, to make notes on. They've probably seen it before. If not, it could look a bit like figure 4.13.

It looks exactly as described, so no surprises there. You might be surprised though by how much you can do with it. If you haven't seen anything like this before, you will probably notice a blank page in student exam question booklets, even if it doesn't explicitly say 'blank page.' However, if you have never seen even one blank page in a question booklet, then it is worth making a special request, on behalf of your students, that a blank piece be made available to them for the exam. What follows is an idea for using it to plan during an exam. If students divide it in four sections, then some sections can be used for the creative writing task, and for making general notes (figure 4.14).

blank page

Figure 4.13

Final Words (for Students)

Up until this point, I've been speaking to the professionals reading this text, so I thought for this final section I would write something specifically for students. To the professional, I encourage you to share the recommendations

Some exams contain a creative writing task. If you have ideas for your writing task or a scaffold for a story plan, then you can jot it down here.

Write any random notes or scribbles here. You might want to use it to draft your 'Argue' question. You might also use it to make notes on literary techniques.

creative writing plan	NOTES

blank page

A:

C: What happens in the text to make me think this?

C: What's the best quote?

E: What technique is in the quote?

S: What might the technique make the viewer think/feel?

S: What's the text saying about the theme?

Quotes

Get down your ACCESS questions so you can follow the process as you write. You can write your 'Argue' question here to keep you focused on your essay's purpose.

This can be used as a great little reservoir for all those quotes you've memorised. Jot them down as soon as you get the opportunity to write!

Figure 4.14

given and support students to implement a routine around exam preparation and planning. As previously mentioned, there are sample goals in the Appendix, but you could also shape some of the content which follows into goals. Ask your students what they think, so you can get some feedback on their priorities for improving their own learning.

Students. . .

Practise! Make sure you know your scaffolds and strategies and have practised them by analysing your texts. Write essays under timed conditions using a blank page to plan.

★

Stick to the habit of writing your body paragraphs first, even in exams. All you need to do is start your first body paragraph further down the page, leaving anywhere from the first 5–8 lines blank. If you have practised writing your essay, you'll know how many lines you generally need for your introductions. If you're not sure, leave a space the length of your index finger.

★

You won't have time to fill the ACCESS tables, so write a copy of the questions. Answer the questions in sequence, writing them straight into your answer booklet as a paragraph. Again, practise this, so you nail it!

★

Lastly, make sure your quotes are easier to remember. The shorter the better. If you have long quotes, then trim them down. Choose quotes that contain literary techniques also—you'll get more bang for your buck because the quotes will serve a dual purpose. If you want to use a longer quote because it contains more than one essential thought, then use elliptical punctuation to make it shorter:

> "You should not have believed me, for virtue cannot so inoculate our old stock but we shall relish of it. I loved you not."

Might become:

> "You should not have believed me. . . . I loved you not."

★

Don't forget to make the most of any blank pages in question booklets or spare paper provided by examiners. Jot down anything on the blank page that you think you might forget, especially quotes.

★

Don't be afraid to take the time to plan before you write. Even if you have 40 minutes allocated for your essay, taking 5–10 minutes scrawling quotes, writing ACCESS questions, breaking down your topic and producing an Argue question will pay off.

Better this than twisting your pen nervously between your fingers for 20 minutes 'thinking,' or writing a lot of irrelevant stuff because you're desperate to get pen to paper. I would rather run out of time and finish with three solid body paragraphs, instead of a long introduction and a body paragraph.

Don't panic. If you practise, you'll have time to finish.

Trust the process!

References

Graham, S., & Perin, D. (2007). A meta-analysis of writing instruction for adolescent students. *Journal of Educational Psychology, 99*(3), 445–476. https://doi.org/10.1037/0022-0663.99.3.445

Lowry, L. (2008). *The giver*. Harper Collins.

Appendix

Text-type, Genre, Theme Definitions

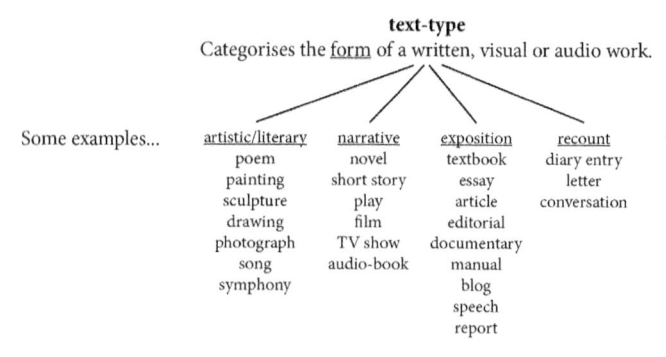

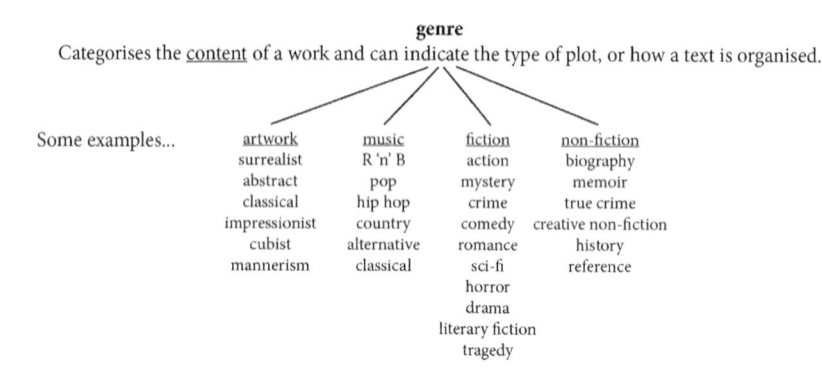

text-type
Categorises the <u>form</u> of a written, visual or audio work.

Some examples...

artistic/literary	narrative	exposition	recount
poem	novel	textbook	diary entry
painting	short story	essay	letter
sculpture	play	article	conversation
drawing	film	editorial	
photograph	TV show	documentary	
song	audio-book	manual	
symphony		blog	
		speech	
		report	

genre
Categorises the <u>content</u> of a work and can indicate the type of plot, or how a text is organised.

Some examples...

artwork	music	fiction	non-fiction
surrealist	R 'n' B	action	biography
abstract	pop	mystery	memoir
classical	hip hop	crime	true crime
impressionist	country	comedy	creative non-fiction
cubist	alternative	romance	history
mannerism	classical	sci-fi	reference
		horror	
		drama	
		literary fiction	
		tragedy	

theme
The topics covered and explored in a text (the message is the interpretation of the themes):
The themes indicate what a text is about.

Some examples...

addiction	commerce	family	identity	memory	rebirth	success
adolescence	commitment	fate	illness	mental health	regrets	suffering
aging	community	feminism	incarceration	money	relationships	survival
alienation	doubt	food	individual	mortality	rejection	terrorism
ambition	dying	freedom	innocence	nature	religion	time
animals	deception	friendship	isolation	nostalgia	reputation	tradition
apocalypse	depression	fulfillment	journeys	obsessions	responsibility	travel
art	disability	futility	joy	oppression	revenge	utopia/dystopia
battles	disillusion	gambling	justice	parenting	rites of passage	violence
beast within	discovery	gender	knowledge	peace	sacrifice	war
beauty	education	grief	life	politics	science	wisdom
belonging	environment	guilt	loneliness	postmodernity	sexuality	women
birth	evil	heroism	loss	power	social status	work
change	exile	Holocaust (The)	love	prejudice	society	youth
cheating	experience	hope	marriage	pride	spiritualism	
childhood	faith	humanity	masculinity	race	strength	

Worksheet A.1

Sample Goals for Individual Learning Plans

The following goals are examples, and not all these goals would go in a plan for one student. You might choose a few depending on a student's needs, then adjust the conditions of the goal or even specify any additional scaffolding the student receives. Timelines (end of term 2, for example) environment (in the classroom, at home etc.) and level of support (with mild, moderate or heavy prompting) are examples of conditions that can change as students progress and the goals are adjusted.

Main Goal

For _____ to analyse texts to plan and write an English essay applying scaffolded supports with mild/moderate/heavy prompting or independently, in the classroom/at home/during exams.

Sub Goals

A) To apply scaffolds and strategies that support identifying and expressing the <u>main idea</u> in a text.

    To identify themes in a <u>short story/chapter/novel/poem</u> with ___% success on three consecutive occasions by the end of term ___.

    To express 'what the text is saying about the theme' with ___% success on three consecutive occasions by the end of term ___.

B) To apply scaffolds and strategies that support <u>understanding essay topics and planning an essay.</u>

    To deconstruct an essay topic successfully with ___% success on three consecutive occasions by the end of term ___.

    Formulating a body paragraph 'Assert' question with ___% success on three consecutive occasions by the end of term ___.

        Using a basic topic strategy.
        Using an agree/disagree topic strategy.
        Using a divide and conquer topic strategy.
        Using an incorporate topic strategy.

    To recall the essay planning scaffold with ___% success on three consecutive occasions by the end of term ___.

    To recall the ACCESS scaffold questions with ___% success on three consecutive occasions by the end of term ___.

    To recall the PREP scaffold questions with ___% success on three consecutive occasions by the end of term ___.

    To recall the PS scaffold questions with ___% success on three consecutive occasions by the end of term ___.

C) To apply scaffolds and strategies that support <u>writing clear sentences.</u>

- To identify appropriate themes and nouns to start a sentence with ___% success on three consecutive occasions by the end of term ___.
- To identify appropriate verbs to animate nouns with ___% success on three consecutive occasions by the end of term ___.
- To combine sentences using appropriate conjunctions with ___% success on three consecutive occasions by the end of term ___.
- To write clear sentences in an essay paragraph with ___% success on three consecutive occasions by the end of term ___.

D) To apply scaffolds and strategies that support <u>writing an essay.</u>

- To write a **body paragraph** with ___% success on three consecutive occasions by the end of term ___.
  - To argue something by formulating a point with ___% success on three consecutive occasions by the end of term ___.
  - To clarify a point with ___% success on three consecutive occasions by the end of term ___.
  - To quote to support assertions with ___% success on three consecutive occasions by the end of term ___.
  - To extract a technique from a text with ___% success on three consecutive occasions by the end of term ___.
  - To scrutinise a text's language and techniques with ___% success on three consecutive occasions by the end of term ___.
  - To synthesise a body paragraph argument with ___% success on three consecutive occasions by the end of term ___.
- To write an essay **introduction** with ___% success on three consecutive occasions by the end of term ___.
  - To paraphrase the essay topic with ___% success on three consecutive occasions by the end of term ___.
  - To respond to the essay topic with ___% success on three consecutive occasions by the end of term ___.
  - To explain the response to an essay topic with ___% success on three consecutive occasions by the end of term ___.
  - To present all essay points with ___% success on three consecutive occasions by the end of term ___.
- To write a **conclusion** with ___% success on three consecutive occasions by the end of term ___.
  - To polish a response to the essay topic with ___% success on three consecutive occasions by the end of term ___.
  - To summarise all that has been synthesised in the body paragraphs with ___% success on three consecutive occasions by the end of term ___.

Some Oral Language Supports

<u>Supporting Expressive Language</u>

Recasting what is said:

 Did you mean. . .?
 Does that mean. . .?
 Good! So what you're saying is. . .?
 Great! So you mean. . .?

Provide binary choice:

 Do you think _____ or_____?
 Maybe _____ or _____?
 So are you saying _____ or_____?

When necessary, hold up each hand to represent the choices, so students can also point if they don't wish to speak.

<u>Supporting Receptive Language</u>

Cue/Orient listeners:

 Class. . .
 Everyone. . .
 First, we will . . . read/write/take/go/put . . .

Provide chronological instructions (avoid before/after):

 First. . .
 Second. . .
 Next. . .
 Last. . .

For instructions, lead with concrete verbs to keep sentences simple and clear:

 Take. . .
 Get. . .
 Fold. . .
 Read. . .
 Summarise. . .
 Write. . .

Text + Theme Schemas

Text + Theme Schema
BASIC SCHEMA

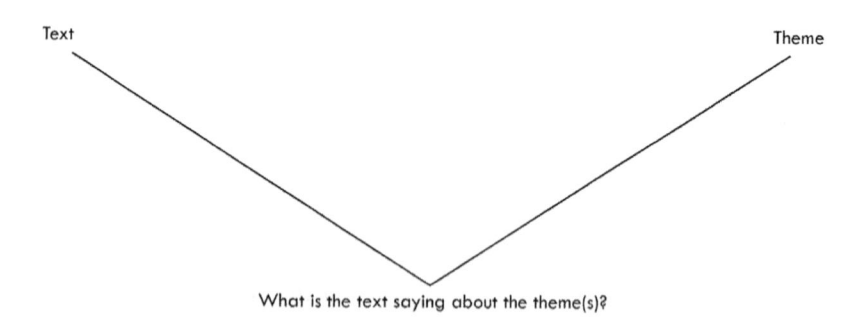

Text   Theme

What is the text saying about the theme(s)?

Worksheet A.2

Text + Theme Schema
EXTENDED 'SCAFFOLDED' SCHEMA

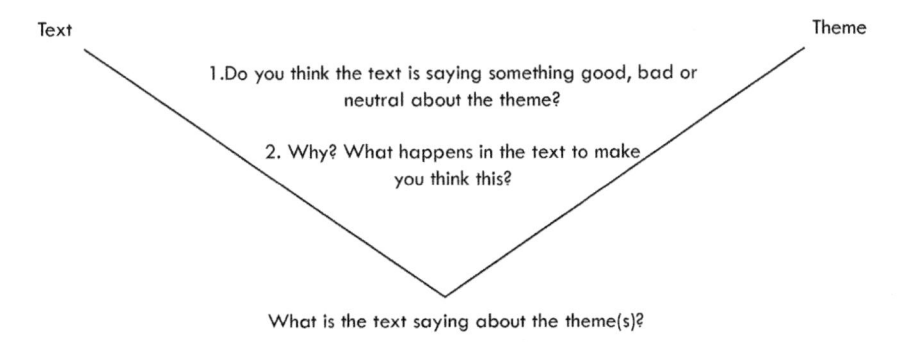

Text   Theme

       1.Do you think the text is saying something good, bad or neutral about the theme?

       2. Why? What happens in the text to make you think this?

What is the text saying about the theme(s)?

Worksheet A.3

Text + Theme Schema
DEFINING STRATEGY

Define your theme or area of study

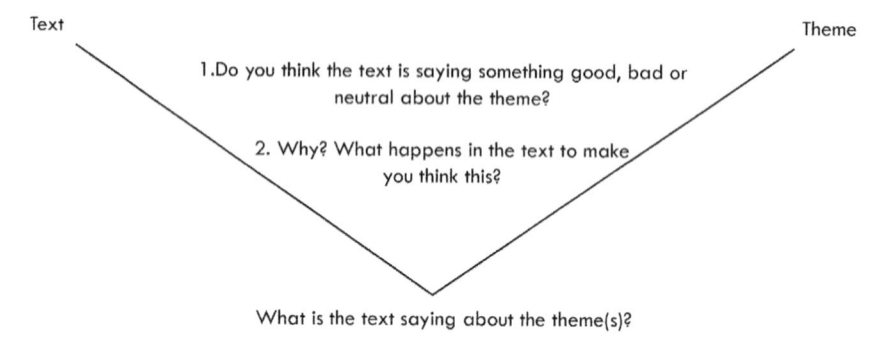

Text   Theme

1. Do you think the text is saying something good, bad or neutral about the theme?

2. Why? What happens in the text to make you think this?

What is the text saying about the theme(s)?

Worksheet A.4

Text + Theme' Schema
PAIRS STRATEGY

Text   Theme

1. Do you think the text is saying something good, bad or neutral about the theme?

2. Why? What happens in the text to make you think this?

What is the text saying about the theme(s)?

_____ & _____

_____ & _____

_____ & _____

Worksheet A.5

'Text + Theme' Schema
SYNTACTIC SCAFFOLD

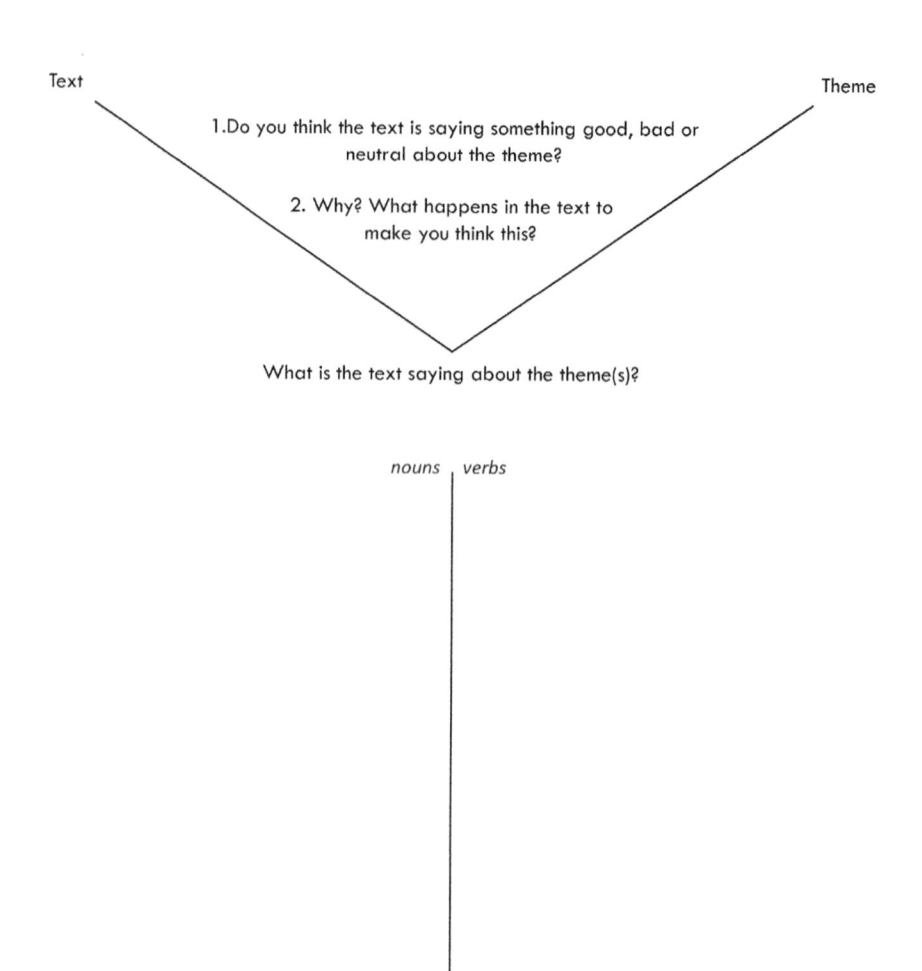

Text Theme

1. Do you think the text is saying something good, bad or neutral about the theme?

2. Why? What happens in the text to make you think this?

What is the text saying about the theme(s)?

nouns | verbs

Worksheet A.6

'Text + Theme' Schema
CUMULATIVE STRATEGY

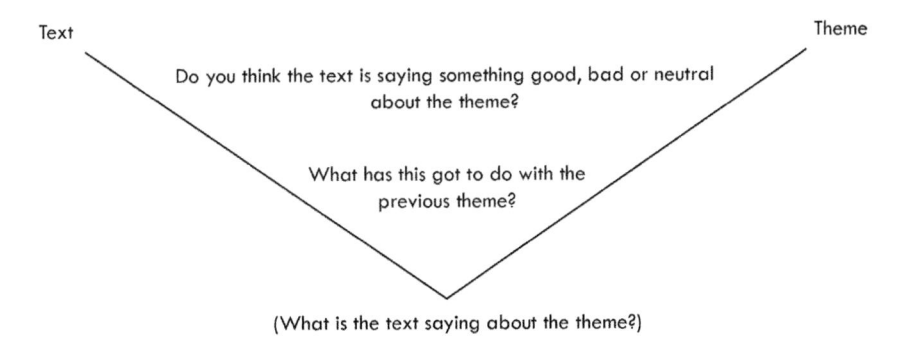

Text   Theme

Do you think the text is saying something good, bad or neutral about the theme?

What has this got to do with the previous theme?

(What is the text saying about the theme?)

Worksheet A.7

116 *Appendix*

Basic Narrative Schema

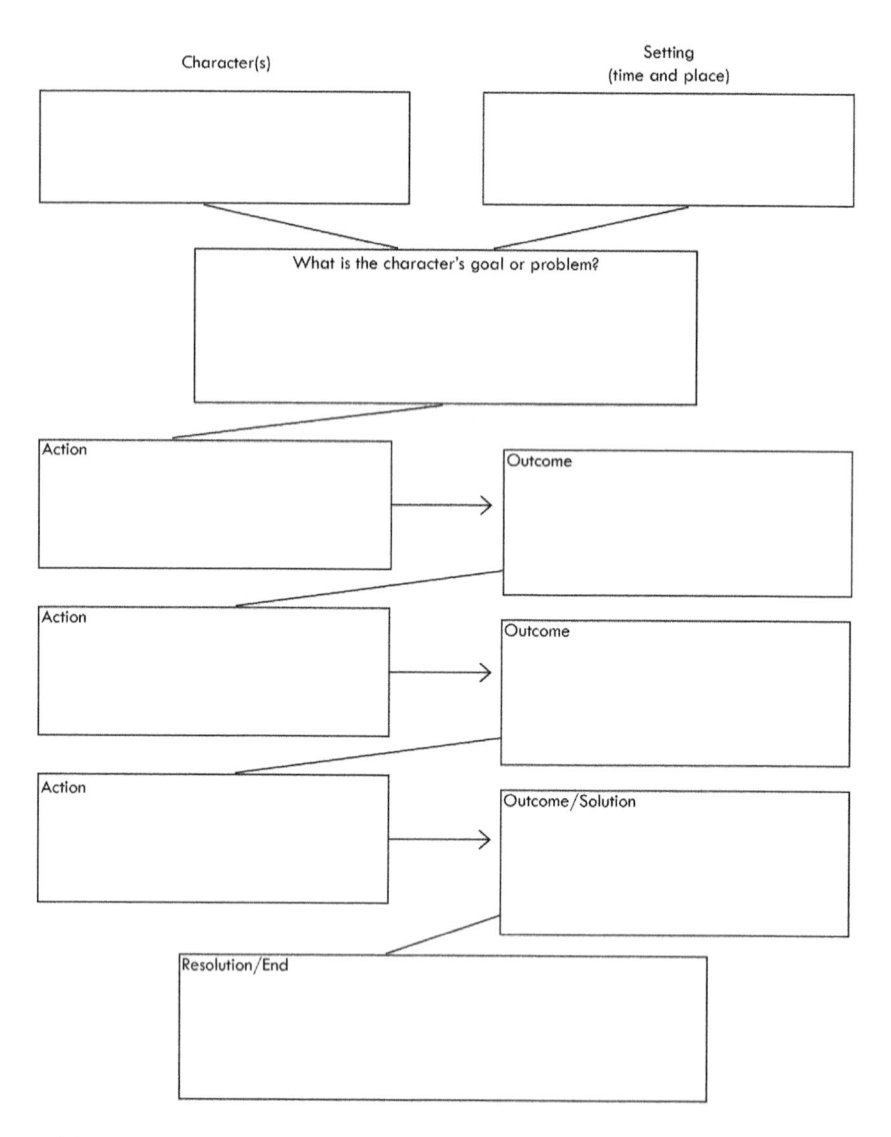

Character(s)

Setting
(time and place)

What is the character's goal or problem?

Action → Outcome

Action → Outcome

Action → Outcome/Solution

Resolution/End

Worksheet A.8

Cause and Effect Schema

Do you think the text might be saying something good, bad, or neutral about the theme? *I think the text is saying...*
Which event are you thinking of? *I'm thinking of the part where...*
Which characters are involved?
What do they want? *They want...*
What do they do? *So they...*
What is the consequence? *Because...*
Why is this good, bad or neutral? *Therefore...*

Worksheet A.9

Body Paragraph ACCESS Scaffold

Argue: What is one
Clarify: What happens in the text to make you think this? In the text…
Confirm: What is the best example (quote)? For example…
Extract technique: Is there a technique in the quote or elsewhere? The author uses…
Scrutinise: What might the technique make the viewer *think* or *feel*? The _____ makes the viewer think/feel/imagine…   technique
Synthesise: What is the text saying about the theme? The text shows…

Worksheet A.10

PREP Introduction Scaffold

Paraphrase: What's your fluffy first sentence? (OPTIONAL)
Respond: What is your short answer/response to the essay topic?
Explain: Is there anything to clarify for your reader? definitions? etc. (OPTIONAL)
Points: What are your body paragraph Arguments?

Worksheet A.11

PS Conclusion Scaffold

Place all answers to 'synthesise' questions in the table below.

Synthesise 1:
Synthesise 2:
Synthesise 3:
Synthesise 4 (optional):

Polish: Can you restate and refine your overall response to the topic?
Summarise what you've synthesised: What do these observations have in common? Ultimately, the text shows...

Worksheet A.12

Pronouns

PERSON	SUBJECT	OBJECT	DETERMINER	POSSESSIVE	REFLEXIVE
singular					
first	I	me	my	mine	myself
second	you	you	your	yours	yourself
third	he, she, it	him, her, it	his, her, its	his, hers, its	himself, herself, itself
plural					
first	we	us	our	ours	ourselves
second	you	you	your	yours	yourselves
third	they	them	their	theirs	themselves

Worksheet A.13

Verb Tenses

Of all the word classes, verbs are among the trickiest to explain. Here, they're divided into being, doing, and helper words. Helper verbs assist being and doing verbs to alter plural, past tense, and other stuff. All groups, except Helper 2 words, can be the sole verb in a sentence (*I can* is an elliptical sentence; it implies another verb: *I can [swim]*, for example).

This list is not exhaustive, it's just for students to get a feel for how verbs can be combined to shape meaning.

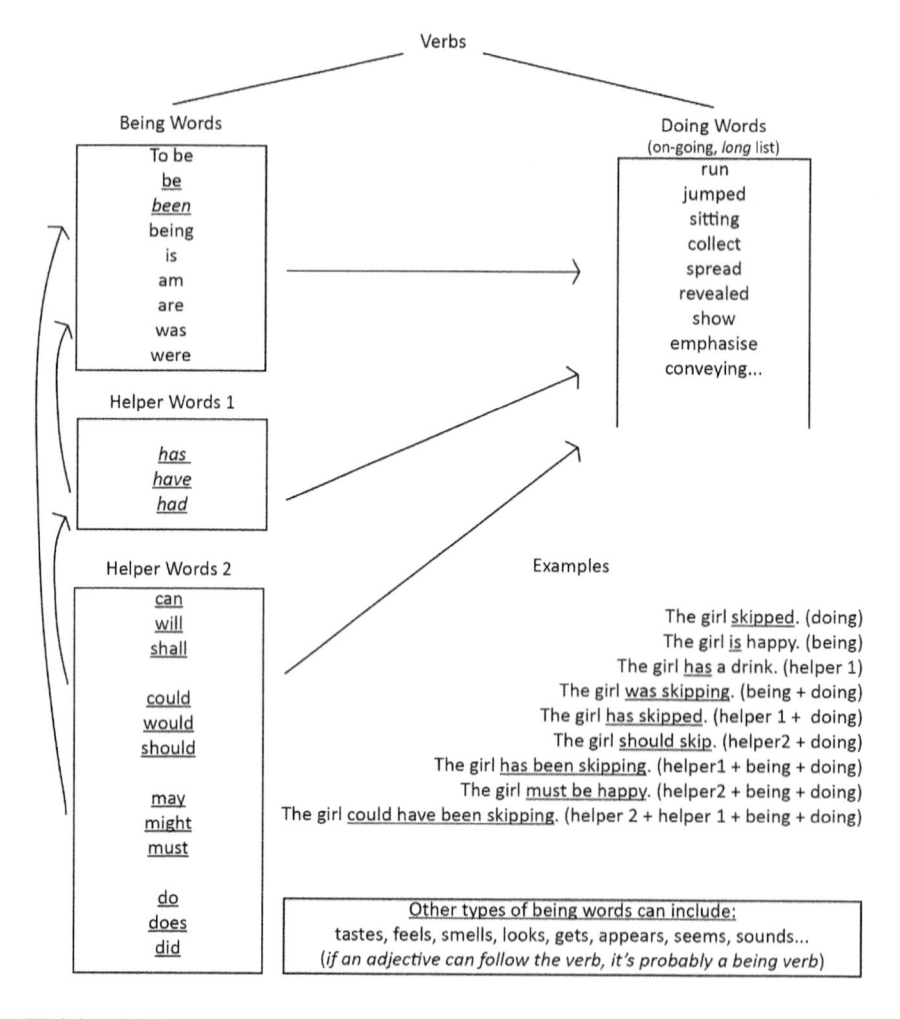

Verbs

Being Words

To be
- be
- been
- being
- is
- am
- are
- was
- were

Doing Words (on-going, *long* list)
- run
- jumped
- sitting
- collect
- spread
- revealed
- show
- emphasise
- conveying...

Helper Words 1
- has
- have
- had

Helper Words 2
- can
- will
- shall

- could
- would
- should

- may
- might
- must

- do
- does
- did

Examples

The girl <u>skipped</u>. (doing)
The girl <u>is</u> happy. (being)
The girl <u>has</u> a drink. (helper 1)
The girl <u>was skipping</u>. (being + doing)
The girl <u>has skipped</u>. (helper 1 + doing)
The girl <u>should skip</u>. (helper2 + doing)
The girl <u>has been skipping</u>. (helper1 + being + doing)
The girl <u>must be happy</u>. (helper2 + being + doing)
The girl <u>could have been skipping</u>. (helper 2 + helper 1 + being + doing)

Other types of being words can include:
tastes, feels, smells, looks, gets, appears, seems, sounds...
(*if an adjective can follow the verb, it's probably a being verb*)

Worksheet A.14

Incorporated Strategy Synonyms

Terms for the topic breakdown strategy

The following groups of words can help you determine what parts of your essay topic may already be part of the ACCESS structure. If you need to, use a thesaurus to expand the list.

Clarify
demonstrate, explain, show, illustrate, make clear, outline, elucidate

Confirm
give examples, provide quotes, provide evidence, prove, support, give substance, justify, substantiate, verify, authenticate

Extract technique
discuss techniques, support with literary techniques, examine techniques, discuss language techniques, look at techniques, discuss language used

Scrutinise
analyse, investigate, probe, interpret, evaluate

Synthesise
summarise, sum-up, conclude

Worksheet A.15

Selection of Summarised Texts

The Giver

By Lois Lowry

The Giver is about a boy who lives in a utopian community where war and pain are things of the past, a society devoid of the problems that can come with emotions. The community is highly regulated with limited choice. When members of the community turn twelve, they are assigned a job. Husbands and wives are also assigned to each other, and are assigned babies. Language is different in this community: Babies are Newchildren, Released is what happens to the elderly or imperfect Newchildren, and Elsewhere is beyond the community boundaries.

Jonas has a younger sister, Lily. His father works nurturing Newchildren, and his mother works in justice. From early on we see that Jonas stands out in the community; among other notable differences, he looks different, he can see some things in colour, where the rest of the community sees only black and white, and he also feels pain. When Jonas turns twelve, he is assigned his occupation at a ceremony. He is assigned the job, Receiver of Memory.

The Receiver of Memories keeps the community's memories to protect them from pain and suffering, but the memories are also kept by the Receiver so that past mistakes won't be repeated. The former Receiver must transfer his memories to Jonas. He is known as the Giver. Some memories Jonas receives are painful, others pleasant. As Jonas starts to feel more things, he realises how empty people's lives are without memories, emotion and choice. The Giver feels the same way and encourages Jonas's growing opposition to the ways of the community.

Jonas learns that Gabriel, a Newchild his father is nurturing, will be Released. When Jonas learns that Released means the child will die, the Giver and Jonas devise a plan to change things. Jonas plans to leave the community and enter the outside world of Elsewhere. Once there, his memories will be released back into the community. The Giver agrees to stay behind and help the people understand the confusing memories that will flood back.

When Jonas learns Gabriel is to be released sooner than expected, he takes Gabriel and flees the community. Jonas discovers that the outside world is harsh, and he struggles to protect Gabriel and survive the tough environment. Eventually Jonas finds a sled in the snow, a sled from one of his memories, and he rides it with Gabriel down towards a village.

Burial Rites

By Hannah Kent

The story is set in the 1820s, in Iceland. Agnes has been convicted of murder along with two other conspirators, Fridrik and Sigga, and is sentenced to death. Instead of going to prison, Agnes is sent to stay with a family. A Reverend called Toti, is appointed spiritual advisor to Agnes.

The family—Officer Jon, his wife Margret and their two daughters—are not happy with the decision and are unkind to Agnes when she arrives. The neighbours are also harsh and unsympathetic.

Agnes helps around the house and garden, doing chores assigned to her. As she becomes closer to Toti, she reveals more about her life, and Toti learns more about Agnes's past. She tells the Reverend about her childhood, how her mother abandoned her, and how her foster mother died, and how she knows she has a sibling but doesn't know where they are.

Toti is compassionate and discusses Agnes's case with District Commissioner Blondal. Blondal is unsympathetic and tries to convince Toti not to trust her, but Toti is only more convinced that maybe Agnes might not be as guilty as he had thought. Margret also becomes more sympathetic and attached to Agnes and will miss her when she is executed. Margret's daughter is disgusted by this closeness.

Agnes reveals to Toti how she met Natan, the man she is convicted of murdering. She fell in love with Natan and accepted an invitation to move in and become his housekeeper, but Sigga, 15, and one of the conspirators, was already living there and was also Natan's lover. Agnes reveals how violent Natan became in the last few days of his life and how he told her to leave the house when she questioned him about Sigga.

It is revealed that Fridrik was responsible for bashing Natan with a hammer. Natan was in pain and close to death when Agnes found him. She killed him to end the pain, then burned the house to conceal the crime.

On the day of her execution, Margret and her family tell her how much she will be missed and dress her for the execution. The story ends with Agnes frightened, declaring she is not ready to die. The epilogue reveals that Agnes is executed and buried with no observed rites.

Maestro

By Peter Goldsworthy

The story begins when young Paul and his family move to Darwin. Paul's parents, who are both musicians, are keen to sign Paul up for piano lessons with the local tutor, Herr Eduard Keller.

Paul starts at his new school and develops a crush on a classmate, Megan, however she is not interested in Paul. During his first few piano lessons, Keller does not let Paul play, instead Paul watches Keller play and talk about music. Paul starts at his new school and gets bullied. He retreats to the music room where he practises. Eventually, Paul is allowed to play the old piano while Keller continues to play the grand piano which is in pristine condition.

While visiting Adelaide for Christmas, Paul digs around in the library and finds information on a couple who could be Keller and his wife. Keller's wife is said to be a famous Jewish classical vocalist, and Keller is listed as having died in 1944.

At school, Paul meets a new student called Rosie. Rosie accompanies Paul to the music room. At first Paul is disinterested, but he comes around after the two of them attend a concert together.

Paul joins a rock band at school, and they enter a battle of the bands competition. They win a trip to Adelaide to compete in the finals. While he is there, Paul enters a piano competition and Keller accompanies him to Adelaide to play the second piano for Paul's competition piece. Eventually the band split and go their separate ways.

While in Adelaide, Paul notices a faded blue tattoo on Keller's arm. Keller dismisses Paul's questions about this. Paul places third in the piano competition.

After high school, Paul leaves Darwin to study Law and music. Music quickly dominates his studies. Paul travels the world chasing his dream and entering piano competitions. Paul tracks down an old acquaintance of Keller's who believes that Keller is dead. The friend tells Paul that Keller played for Hitler to save himself and his wife, but this backfired and they went to a concentration camp anyway.

Paul ends up in Melbourne, where he teaches piano and marries Rosie. He visits Keller during his last days in a home. When Keller dies, Paul's hopes and dreams die with him.

The Shoe-Horn Sonata

By John Misto

Bridie, an Australian Nurse, and Sheila, who is British, were prisoners of war in a Japanese camp during World War II. It's fifty years on and they are appearing in a documentary.

While fleeing Singapore, Bridie tells her interviewer how her ship was torpedoed, and she was captured by the Japanese. Sheila was also on a ship that was bombed. Sheila and Bridie were both held in the same prisoner of war camp.

The two women have not seen each other since the camp. Sheila lived in Australia in the intervening years and, back at the hotel, Bridie tells Sheila that she is upset that Sheila never reached out to her. Sheila is unapologetic. She is also very conservative and has doubts about the documentary, thinking that maybe they shouldn't share their story so openly.

Bridie tells the interviewer that she and other women at the camp avoided becoming part of a Japanese brothel by pretending to have tuberculosis. Sheila tells the interviewer that the Japanese got the idea for the brothel from one of the Australian soldiers. Bridie shoots back that the British women received special treatment in exchange for sleeping with the Japanese soldiers.

The women also relay a story of how they coped in the camp by starting a choir. Bridie had a shoe-horn her father had given her when she went off to war, and she used this to tap the rhythm while the others sang.

While drunk at the hotel, Sheila tells Bridie that she didn't want to remember the camp and that's why she never contacted Bridie after the war. Sheila reveals she has Bridie's shoe-horn and shows it to her. Sheila tells Bridie that she didn't trade it for medicine when Bridie was sick in the camp, but instead slept with a soldier in exchange for the medicine she needed. Sheila thinks

Bridie would not have done this for her because Bridie said she would never have slept with a Japanese soldier for anyone. Bridie confesses that she was arrested for shoplifting; she accidentally ran out of a shop with items she was holding because she heard people speaking Japanese and this frightened her. Both women realise they are still deeply affected by the war.

In the interview they reveal each other's secrets and liberate themselves from their mental confines. They celebrate by dancing together back at the hotel; something they vowed to do after the war but never did.

The Arrival

By Shaun Tan

A man flees his home in an unidentified foreign land, under the shadow of an ominous serpent. He's bound for somewhere safe to resettle. He leaves his family behind in the hope of finding work in a new country, then sending for them later.

The man travels by sea with many other people, presumably in the same position. There are many obstacles: bureaucracy and language barriers are just the start.

When he arrives, the land is strange and so are the creatures. As he attempts to establish himself in this new place, he meets other immigrants along the way, and they share their stories. They relay their own unique tales of adversity and the tribulation of leaving their homes and emigrating.

A young woman shares her story of escape from enslavement and forced labour. A man tells the story of how his homeland was invaded by giants, and how he escaped with his partner, at first hiding underground and then leaving by boat.

The man finds a job delivering parcels that doesn't work out. Then he finds work on a factory production line, where he discards faulty items. Here he befriends an old man who reveals the horrors he endured as a young soldier. The old man tells him how he returned home from war injured, only to find his town in tatters.

With accommodation and a job, the man writes to his family and receives a reply. The man's family arrive safely and they start their new life.

Copy of Fairy Tales

Little Red Riding Hood

Once upon a time, in a little shack on the edge of a dark forest lived a little girl. One day she decided to visit her ailing grandmother. Grandma lived far away, and the only path was through the dark woods. The girl's father packed some food. Her mother gave her a red, hooded cape for the cold journey, then the little girl set off through the forest.

After a time, she stopped to rest. As she sat, the bushes rustled. A wolf appeared, raised on his back legs. Startled, the little girl jumped, dropping her basket.

"Don't be afraid," said the wolf. "I won't harm you." The wolf looked at the basket. "What's in there?"

"None of your business," she replied, snatching up her basket.

The wolf frowned, "No need to be rude. I was just curious. These woods are lonely. I only meant to acquaint myself with you in the hope of some polite conversation, but never mind." The wolf turned to leave.

"Wait," said the little girl. "I don't mean to be impolite." The wolf turned and smiled. She continued, "I have food in the basket, for my grandma. She is old and ill and I am on my way to her now."

"Oh," said the wolf, "I'm sorry to hear your grandma is ill. Have you travelled far to see her?"

"Yes, but I still have a way to go, yet!"

"How far exactly?"

The little girl explained to the wolf exactly how far, and where, she had to go. The wolf shook his head. "That does sound like a long way. You'd best be off then. Thank you for the conversation." And with that, the little girl waved the wolf goodbye and continued her journey. "What a nice wolf," she thought.

When the little girl arrived at grandma's house, the door was already open. Fearing the worst, she rushed inside and to her relief, found grandma safely tucked into bed—but she looked different. "Grandma, what big eyes you have." said the little girl.

"All the better to see you with," replied grandma.

"And your ears are bigger too!"

"All the better to hear you with my darling."

The little girl gasped, "and how your teeth have grown!"

"All the better to eat you with," said grandma, only it wasn't grandma. The wolf sprung up from under the sheets and launched himself across the room.

After a time, the room fell silent. The wolf licked his paws then adjusted his bonnet. A loud burp escaped from his mouth. He patted his full belly. 'Two big meals in one day,' contemplated the wolf, "I'd best have some rest before I see what's on the menu tomorrow," and with that he lay down on the bed and thumbed the label on the red hooded cape. It said, 'If found please return to 25 Meadow Lane.' The wolf grinned a vicious grin.

Little Blue Riding Boots

Once upon a time, in a little shack on the edge of a dark forest lived a little girl. One day she decided to visit her ailing grandmother. Grandma lived far away, and the only path was through the dark woods. The girl's father packed some food. Her mother gave her a pair of blue boots for the rough journey, then the little girl set off through the forest.

After a time, the girl stopped to rest. As she sat, the bushes rustled. A wolf appeared, raised on his back legs. Startled, the little girl jumped, dropping her basket.

"Don't be afraid," said the wolf. "I won't harm you." The wolf looked at the basket. "What's in there?"

"None of your business," she replied, snatching up her basket.

The wolf frowned, "No need to be rude. I was just curious. These woods are lonely. I only meant to acquaint myself with you in the hope of some polite conversation, but never mind." The wolf turned to leave.

"Wait," said the little girl. "I do not mean to be impolite." The wolf turned and smiled. She continued, "I have food in the basket, for my grandma. She is old and ill and I am on my way to her now."

"Oh," said the wolf, "I'm sorry to hear your grandma is ill. Have you travelled far to see her?"

"Yes, but I still have a way to go, yet!"

"How far exactly?"

The little girl explained to the wolf exactly how far, and where, she had to go. The wolf shook his head. "That does sound like a long way. You'd best be off then. Thank you for the conversation." And with that, the little girl waved the wolf goodbye and continued her journey. "What a nice wolf," she thought.

When the little girl arrived at grandma's house, the door was already open. Fearing the worst, she rushed inside and to her relief, found grandma sitting at the table sipping hot chocolate, and there, opposite her, sat the wolf with a mug in his hand.

"Come in darling! I have some great news." said grandma. "This lovely wolf is a rich philanthropist. When you told him I was unwell, he came to visit. When I told him about my expensive medical bills, he offered to pay them."

The wolf smiled at the little girl, "you must care very much about your grandma to travel so far, all alone, and for that I would also like to move your grandma closer to you, so you can all be together."

The little girl didn't know what to say, she was so overcome with joy. She ran and embraced her grandmother. The wolf smiled. They drank tea and ate biscuits. And they all lived happily ever after.

Short Stories for Extra Practice

Mastering Technology

The new phone finally arrived. Tyler unwrapped it, and marveled at its newness, all sleek and shiny in his hand. He turned it on and swiped, pressed, clicked and typed his way to the home screen—it was finally ready to use. He opened the app store and commenced his first task: to find the best diary application he could.

His first part-time job had been at the supermarket, stacking shelves. After he'd graduated high school, he'd worked at a car dealership for a man who smelled of stale cigarettes and yelled if Tyler was a minute late. He'd dreamed of running his own business one day, and now it was happening.

He was his own boss, and if he was going to start off on the right foot, he had to get organised. He swiped-up through the list of apps, mouthing silently, skimming the names, features and reviews, then found it: *Schedule Me!*

According to the description, *Schedule Me!* planned everything: to do lists, meetings, calls, what to buy, what to wear, when to take a break—it even monitored your steps, heartbeat and sleep. It was the ultimate corporate tool. Tyler hit download.

★★★

The young doctor flashed her pen torch into the patient's eyes: nothing, no dilation, not even a flinch when she pinched his skin. She could hardly hear or feel his breath, but the heart monitor was pinging. He was alive, just comatose.

When this happened to the young ones, it was always the corporate types, she thought as she wrote in Tyler Caruthers's file. If it wasn't burn-out, it was mental exhaustion, but this was worse. They'd wheeled him in on Saturday, his whole body shaking, eyes glazed, mumbling about tasks, and to dos, about schedules, before he'd passed out. All that ambition and what did these people have to show for it? They became slaves to their jobs. This young man would never be the same again. Poor guy.

She looked at her watch to mark the time and wrote it down. Damn! It was after 6pm. She wanted to see the head of psychiatry before he left for the day; it was about that promotion. Something buzzed on the table. It was a phone. She cocked her head. She could have sworn her patient's belongings were locked in the drawer. She looked at the screen: it was a reminder to talk to Dr. Grant, the psychiatrist, tomorrow. She gasped, then it buzzed again; another message appeared demanding she stay calm and watch her heart rate . . . and it knew her name.

The young doctor smiled to herself as she slipped the phone into her pocket. She'd figure out who had pranked her later. In the meantime, she'd keep the little phone. It might prove quite useful.

Fun Run

She smiled at me! The nerve! Standing there at the starting line with her sunlit skin, short shorts and tank top. The heat's sweltering and she's not even sweating. I'm ugly when I sweat. I go all red, and get wet patches in all the wrong places, but today I don't care. I'm winning this thing.

Yesterday, in the staffroom, she'd asked me to sponsor her. And I did. I pledged $10 if she won. There's only a small group of us running, five or so. I checked my sponsor book, but she hadn't written a thing, not a cent. Ralph from the accounts department was chortling like a pig with a truffle stuck up its nose, spluttering everywhere while he laughed. He was chatting to her—oh, she's so witty, so charming! I'd reached for a biscuit, there were just crumbs on the plate. I looked around, she'd had the last one. Oreo cookies, my favourite. Just typical!

The gun cracks in my ears, and I bolt. Sun, sweat and loose strands of hair blind me. I catch glimpses of everyone else in front, and then nobody. I'm winning! My legs are numb, but still pumping hard, animated by the thought of her face at the end, that glorious misery in her eyes, and. . .

Then I'm down, clutching my knee. I look up, and there she is, by my side, a slender silhouette against the sun asking in that mellifluous voice if I am all right.

It's in the local paper: A photo of her helping me onto a gurney. It's in the article that everyone is donating a portion of their wage to the charity. A record sum. And all because she'd stopped racing to help me. She was coming second, apparently. She could have won if she'd kept going. And she'd raised the most for the win, the most by $10. Typical!

Bliss

They'd been in their new apartment for a week when it started.

There were signs. At first, only little things: relatives from interstate called in the middle of the night panting, then inexplicably hung up. There were stories of pets abandoning their homes, zoo animals breaking free of their enclosures and disappearing. Two weeks later the attacks started and only got worse. People who'd never harmed a soul in their lives were out of control. The streets were unsafe. The news reports came fast: lock your doors, stay inside. The streets were a warzone.

Three weeks in, the television and radio stations stopped broadcasting. A few days later, the power was gone.

Then, a day later, the power was back on. The building's generator came online.

They were warned not to buy an apartment off the plan, not to succumb to the lure of brochures and sales consultants, and the promise of 'resort-style' living. Friends and family gasped when they told them the price and the other charges. But the cost had been worth it, because the expensive building came with an expensive generator, one that was wired to enough solar panels to service every apartment in the boutique block—including the lifts and heated swimming pool.

The rooftop garden was beautiful, and the views were incredible. They planted a veggie patch in the garden, and the space became so much more. It was a place to gather, for residents to forget about the troubles of the world. They collected rainwater and grew grapes for wine. It made them all much closer. They had so much in common.

Two years on, they'd practically forgotten about the zombie apocalypse. Of course, there were still signs it was going on; the ground-floor buttons in the lifts were taped-over, and if they looked down from their stunning glass-fenced balcony for too long, the slow-moving bodies on the street would catch them standing there and would raise their arms, moaning. Sometimes, the people in the apartments waved back. Mostly, they just slipped back into the comfort of their air-conditioned living rooms and helped themselves to more wine.

Two for One

She didn't eat sardines; they were too salty, but 20% off for 20 cans was too good to pass up. Baby beetroots were 2 for 1, and came with a 25% discount voucher for paper towels. She couldn't store beetroots forever, but paper towels would keep.

Her trolley was nearly full, so she pulled over to repack. Meat was cheap. It was close to expiry and on sale. She stacked the five remaining trays of T-bones in her trolley next to the milk. Someone complained to her back. They were mumbling as she rolled away, something about her taking the last of the meat trays. *Too bad*, she thought.

In the tinned vegetables aisle, she scrutinised the tags and, bingo, triple Shopper Points on tinned tomatoes. This would get her the additional 2,000 points for that Business Class flight to Perth. She re-shuffled and loaded the pile of cans into her trolley.

She trundled up to the checkout. *Hello!* magazine was giving away a free gift with purchase. She grabbed a handful and threw them on the conveyer.

She squeezed the loaded grocery bags into her trolley, then swiped two credit cards. Both declined. She thumbed her mum's savings card and wondered if she should call first, to ask mum if she'd mind her using it. She shrugged; mum would appreciate her thriftiness. She whipped out the card and swiped it. It went through.

She packed the car. It barely fit. The garage at home was full, she'd have to reorganise the house, maybe her daughters could share a room?

She returned her trolley to the bay and retrieved the gold coin from the slot on the handle. A man sitting near the trolley stuck his hand out. He stank. She turned away. *Dirty alcoholic*, she groaned under her breath.

Index

ACCESS: paragraph 52, 66, 84, 94; questions 50, 66, 101, 104; scaffold 66, 84, 94–95; schema 47–48, *49*, *51*, 52; worksheets: In the Dark 53; On Display 54; First Impressions 57; The Fish (Yeats) 60; The Four Ages of Man (Yeats) 61; Grief (Barrett Browning) 59; Love (Barrett Browning) 63; No Man is an Island (Donne) 62; Pressure 55; A Singer of the Bush (Paterson) 58; Stalker 56
adolescence 2–3, 11
Anderson, Stavroola A.S. 5
Australia 3–4

Berman, Ruth A. 11
Big Bang Theory 21
Blake, William 49
body paragraph: arguments *92*, *99*; four body-paragraph 100; scaffold (ACCESS) 66, 94–95; three body-paragraph 79, 93, 100
Bransford, John D. 12
Brewer, William F. 11
Burial Rites (Kent) 39, *41*, 80

Collins Cobuild dictionaries 31
conclusions 9, 44, 93–94

deconstruct 28
developmental language disorder 5–6
Dexter, Douglas D. 6
Dockrell, Julie E. 5

essay structure: body paragraph 45, *46*, 64, 66, 91; conclusion scaffold 96–97; English 44, *45*, 64; putting it all together 95; writing, English 91, 101
exams 101

expository: text 5, 11–12
expressive language 6
expressive skills 5

genre 18–19, 21, 52
Giver (Lowry) 33, *34*, 84, 95–96, 98, *99*, *100*
Goldsworthy, Peter 84, 86
Graham, Steve 91

Hamlet (Shakespeare) 65–66, 93
heuristic processes 9
Hughes, Charles A. 6

introductions 45, 91, 93, 103

Johnson, Marcia K. 12

Kent, Hannah 39, 80

Larson, Vicky Lord 11
Lee, Harper 79
Little Red Riding Hood 21, 23, *24*, *25*, *26*, 27
Lord of the Flies 80
Lowry, Lois 33, 96, *99*

Mackie, Clare 5
Maestro (Goldsworthy) 84, 86
Maus (Spiegelman) 42
McKinley, Nancy L. 11
McKinnon, David H. 3
McLeod, Sharynne 3
Midsummer Night's Dream, A 80
memory: declarative/procedural 8; poor 10; working memory 9
Merriam-Webster online 31
meta-analysis 6, 91
micro fiction 52, 64

Index

Nakamura, Glenn V. 11
NAPLAN tests (Australian) 3–4
narrative: scaffolds 17; schemas 11, 17, 51; skills 5; texts 7, 11, 30
Nir-Sagiv, Bracha 11
nouns 5, 35, 38–40

Othello (Shakespeare) 77, 86
Owen, Wilfred 86

Perin, Dolores 91
persuasive text 6–7
PETAL 48
Peterson, Amy K. (et al 2020) 6
Pixar (shorts) 28
Poison Tree, A (Blake) 49, *50*
poems 27, 52
pronouns 74, 77

Rabbits, The 80
receptive language 6
Romeo and Juliet 21, 29, 31, 66, 68, 77

scaffolding 6, 8, 29–30, 42, 46, 96
scaffolds: blank 80, 100; essay 43; narrative 17; visual 7, 12
schema: scaffolded text+theme 29–30, 42, 48; text+theme 21, 23, 25, 52, 94; *see also* exams
sentence: functions (worksheet) 65, 67; starter 24, 30, 33, *35*; structure 1, 6, 38, 44

sentences: inform, instruct, ask 65; multiple 77, 84; writing 2, 8, 13, 39
SEQAL 48
speech pathology 3–4
Spiegelman, Art 42
strategy: agree/disagree 72, 74, 84; basic one way (worksheet) 66, 68, 71; cumulative 42; defining 30–31; divide and conquer 77, 79; incorporate (worksheets) 84, 87–89; pairs 32
Swanson, H. Lee 17

Tan, Shaun 28, 86, 126
text: analysing 2, 12, 25, 91, 103; comprehension 10, 12, 17; construction 5; text-types 18–19, 52
theme: analysing 25; central 79–80; identifying 18, 35, 91; text+theme schema 21, 23, 25, 52, 94
To Kill a Mockingbird (Lee) 79
topic: breakdown 65

verbs: being 36–37, 39–40, 72; doing 36, 39, 72

worksheet: agree/disagree strategy 76; divide and conquer 81–83; essay topics, basic strategy 71; incorporate strategy 87–89; insert negatives 75; sentence function 67; text, theme, genre 20, 78; *see also* ACCESS
World Health Organization (WHO) 3